P-47
THUNDERBOLT
COMBAT MISSIONS

P-47 THUNDERBOLT

COMBAT MISSIONS

FIRST-HAND ACCOUNTS OF
P-47 THUNDERBOLT OPS IN WORLD WAR II

JONATHAN BERNSTEIN

METRO BOOKS
NEW YORK

METRO BOOKS
New York

An Imprint of Sterling Publishing
1166 Avenue of the Americas
New York, NY 10036

METRO BOOKS and the distinctive Metro Books logo are trademarks of Sterling Publishing Co., Inc.

Editorial Director: **Will Steeds**
Project Editor: **Chris McNab**
Designer: **Philip Clucas** MCSD
Photographers: **Jonathan Bernstein, Patrick Bunce**

Jacket and front cover illustration: Roy Grinnell

ISBN: 978-1-4351-5895-5

For information about custom editions, special sales, and premium and corporate purchases, please
contact Sterling Special Sales at 800-805-5489 or specialsales@sterlingpublishing.com

Printed and bound in China

10 9 8 7 6 5 4 3 2 1

Roy Grinnell, Official Artist of the American Fighter Aces Association (AFAA) and the American Combat Airman Hall of Fame (Commemorative Air Force), was an honors graduate of the Art Center School in Los Angeles. He has received many honors and awards, including the R.G. Smith Award for Excellence in Naval Aviation Art, becoming an Honorary Ace of the AFAA, and most recently the opening of the Roy Grinnell Gallery in the American Airpower Heritage Museum (CAF) in Midland, TX. He is also well known for his Western and Native American art. Grinnell's oil paintings have been displayed throughout the world in museums and private collections. His work also features on the covers of *B-24 Combat Missions, B-29 Combat Missions, P-51 Combat Missions,* and *Spitfire: Life of the Legend* (website: www.roygrinnell.com).

www.sterlingpublishing.com

Contents

Introduction

The P-47's evolution from high-altitude escort fighter to nap-of-the-earth "mud mover" and finally to Very Long Range (VLR) strike fighter, is a fascinating study in the adaptability of an extremely well-designed airframe. Improvements in the propeller, engine, fuel capacity, and cockpit visibility all contributed to the Thunderbolt's successes from 1943–45 and made it and the men who flew it a remarkable piece of history.

While the lion's share of the attention paid to the US Army Air Force (USAAF) in World War II went to the strategic bomber crews and the daily missions they flew 30,000ft (9,144m) over enemy territory, the argument can and has been made that the strategic bombing campaign failed in its stated goal of bringing the enemy to his knees by destroying his industry and his ability to wage war. Both Germany and Japan were resilient, and despite the round-the-clock bombing of both nations, their industries continued to increase the production of war materiel as the conflict neared its conclusion.

Fighter escort cover was the key to the bombing campaign, for if the fighters could protect the bombers, the bombers could reach their targets, bomb the enemy, and head for home while the German or Japanese air forces were kept at bay. It was as a fighter escort that the P-47 Thunderbolt first saw combat, 5 miles (8km) above the earth in the rarified air that technology was just enabling airplanes to reach. It was also as a fighter escort that the Thunderbolt's greatest strengths and weaknesses were first realized. The P-47 was a good airplane, but it lacked range to accompany the bombers all the way to Germany and back. Lack of range and a sluggish rate of climb hampered the Thunderbolt through 1943. As famed 4th Fighter Group commander Col. Donald Blakeslee commented after he scored the type's first kill: "It had better be able to dive, because it sure as hell can't climb!"

And dive it could, completely neutralizing the established German escape tactic of diving away from pursuing aircraft, a tactic that had been so effective against the Spitfire and Hurricane. The Thunderbolt's amazing diving ability would become a key element to its second wind as a fighter-bomber as well. Woe to the German pilot who attempted to dive away and disengage, only to find a P-47 still hot on his tail and firing all the way!

Yet it wasn't until the late spring 1944, when new engines and propellers were mated with the Thunderbolt airframe, that the P-47 became a far more potent threat. The new Hamilton Standard and Curtiss Electric paddle blade propellers significantly improved the airplane's rate of climb and completely negated its poorer low-altitude performance.

These improvements were made just as the P-51 was arriving in Europe in significant numbers, and as the newer fighter began to take over the escort mission for the 8th Air Force, the P-47 was being transferred to the 9th Air Force and pressed into the fighter-bomber role. The Thunderbolt not only retained its surprising maneuverability at all altitudes, but it could absorb massive amounts of damage as well, practically shrugging off 20mm cannon fire in many cases. It was not uncommon for a P-47 pilot to take fire, continue his mission, and return home with a rough-running engine, and complete his postflight damage assessment walkaround by finding an entire engine cylinder shot off the airplane. The P-47 was nicknamed the "Jug" (short for Juggernaut) for a very good reason. It took a lot to stop one.

The Jug was the ultimate American fighter of World War II. Although it has been overshadowed by the arguably "sexier" P-51, the Thunderbolt made more aces, flew more missions, dropped more bombs and continually evolved throughout the course of the war, to become a true "multi-role" fighter aircraft. By war's end, the P-47N could fly higher, farther, and faster than the P-51D and it could carry more ordnance while doing it. Gone were the days of "don't get caught below 15,000ft [4,572m] in a P-47," as the Thunderbolt could mix it up from the deck to 30,000ft (9,144m) and beyond and come out the winner. The success of the strategic bombing campaign was not in the destruction of enemy industry, but in that of the enemy air force that challenged the bombers. The degrading of the enemy's tactical airpower allowed the close support and interdiction phases of the air campaign to happen, and that is where the war was won.

P-47 units, along with other Allied fighter-bombers, attacked bridges, rail yards, trains, trucks, armored vehicles, etc. and made it almost impossible for the enemy to move during the daytime. In the last six months of the war, German soldiers had a saying regarding airplanes overhead: "If it is camouflaged, it's British, if it is silver, it's American, if it's not there, it's German." Taking the fight to the enemy fighter force in the air and on the ground ultimately led to the destruction of the enemy's infrastructure and the paralysis of his road network. Once the Germans and Japanese could not resupply their troops on the frontlines with ammunition, food, and medical supplies, defeat was inevitable. Beginning in May 1945, when P-47Ns began operating with near impunity at low altitude over Japan itself, strafing anything of military value that moved, it was clear that Allied victory was secured.

Both the P-47D and P-47N continued to serve after World War II, but by 1947 most Thunderbolts had been replaced by the new jets in active-duty units. There had been talk of sending the Thunderbolt to Korea in 1950, but with Mustangs readily available from stocks mothballed in Japan and the significantly leaner fuel consumption of the now F-51D, the Jug would not see combat, despite a rash of F-51 losses from ground fire that the Thunderbolt would have simply shaken off. The Jug soldiered on in the newly formed Air National Guard until 1955, when the last example was retired.

Jonathan Bernstein

History and Development

"The P-47 is a jack-of-all-trades, and, contrary to tradition, a master of all. The plane was designed originally as a high-altitude fighter, but the exigencies of war brought it downstairs. The Thunderbolt now does dive-bombing, skip-bombing, strafing, and rocket launching as well as high-altitude escort. It does them all superbly well."

—P-47 pilot training manual, 1944

Alexander de Seversky was an airpower visionary. An outstanding pilot, disciple of military aviation pioneer Gen. Billy Mitchell, inventor of several aeronautical systems, pitch man and founder of the Seversky Aircraft Corporation, he did many things well; except run his company so that it made a profit. After the company's second financial bailout in 1938, de Seversky was ousted by the company's board of directors in 1939 and they renamed the company the Republic Aircraft Corporation.

Left: The P-35 was the first all-metal pursuit airplane bought by the Army Air Corps. Seventy-seven P-35s were purchased in 1936.

The company's biggest success with de Seversky at the helm was its contract for seventy-seven SEV-1XP single-seat fighters, which the US Army designated P-35. The Seversky P-35 was the first all-metal modern fighter adopted by the US Army Air Corps (USAAC) and was a significant improvement over the fabric-skinned fighters of the 1920s that remained in service through the early 1930s. The P-35's Pratt & Whitney R1830-45 gave it a top speed of nearly 300mph (482kmh) and a service ceiling of nearly 30,000ft (9,144m).

The first P-35s were purchased in 1936 and hopes were high at Seversky for additional purchases by the USAAC. However, in an effort to sell more airplanes, de Seversky had secretly negotiated a contract with the Japanese for twenty 2PA-B3 two-seat escort fighter variants, which were delivered to the Japanese in late 1937 as the Imperial Japanese Navy's A8V1. With Japanese aggression in China already garnering attention from the US War Department, there was a significant amount

of consternation in the Air Corps over this contract and, as a result, the USAAC chose not to purchase additional P-35s, instead ordering the Curtiss P-36.

With the US arms exportation ban of June 1940, any arms shipments to nations other than England were now considered illegal. As a result of the new embargo, sixty EP-106 (the export variant of the P-35) fighters were seized by the US government and turned over to the USAAC. These sixty aircraft were designated P-35A and were primarily sent to the Philippines, where they equipped the 21st and 34th Fighter Squadrons.

Despite their robust construction, technology had surpassed the P-35A, and without armor and self-sealing fuel tanks the few that did see combat in December 1941 were horribly outclassed by superior Japanese aircraft. All of the type that made it to the Philippines were destroyed by the spring of 1942.

While de Seversky was the company's founder, the soul of the organization could be found in its chief designer and executive vice president, Alexander Kartveli. Kartveli was the driving force behind the Republic design bureau and was responsible for designing every combat aircraft produced by Republic, from the P-35 to the A-10 Thunderbolt II. He viewed aircraft design as an art form and prided himself on creating aesthetically pleasing airplanes.

airplane's vitals, the YP-43 was behind the technological curve. Its good top speed of over 350mph (563kmh) and service ceiling exceeding 35,000ft (10,668m) kept the project alive, however, and resulted in an order for fifty-four production airframes.

As the P-43 entered service, Kartveli continued to improve the design, creating a more advanced variant powered by the 1,400hp R-2180-1 engine, the XP-44 Rocket. Although the design was never adopted, mating the more powerful engine to the robust airframe did increase its performance, showing clear development potential for an even stronger powerplant. As a result, the USAAC decided to wait until the even more powerful 2,000hp R-2800 became available. The planned R-2800 airplane was designated XP-47B, after the original intent for the XP-47 was changed from a lightweight fighter to a high-altitude fighter to accommodate the new engine. As a result, on September 6, 1940, a new contract authorization was issued for the XP-47B. Shortly thereafter, the USAAC ordered 733 P-47B and C model airplanes before the prototype had even flown.

Above: The SEV-3 Amphibian was the first successful airplane design from the Seversky Aircraft Corporation. The first examples were flown in 1933 and broke several amphibian and seaplane speed records.

Right: "Victory Through Air Power" was Alexander de Seversky's analysis of the early years of the war in Europe, written as a lesson in preparedness for the US Army Air Forces.

Kartveli believed the P-35 could be significantly improved, and by 1940 he had redesigned the airframe around the more powerful R1830-35 engine, mated to a General Electric B-2 exhaust-driven supercharger housed in the fuselage. The redesign resulted in a completely new and more streamlined fuselage and a thinner wing with fully inset landing-gear bays. The company-funded AP-4 was a far more aerodynamically "clean" airplane than the P-35, and its performance clearly illustrated the point. Although somewhat less pleasing aesthetically than the current first-line US fighter, the P-40B, the AP-4 had a distinct advantage in speed and altitude over the Curtiss fighter. As a result, the USAAC was interested in evaluating the AP-4, and despite an engine fire that destroyed the original airplane, the Air Corps ordered thirteen examples for evaluation, designating them YP-43.

The first example was delivered in September 1940, and the remaining twelve followed over the next five months. However, combat developments over Europe, occurring just as the first airplane was being accepted, rendered it obsolete before a production order was even placed. Without self-sealing fuel tanks and armor to protect the

Although the XP-47B was Republic's number one priority, manufacture of the P-43 continued, mainly to keep the production line open until it could be converted to produce the P-47B, when the engine production was able to supply powerplants for the new fighter. A handful of P-43s saw service with the USAAC in 1941–42, but the majority went to China as military aid to fight the Japanese. Surprisingly, the P-43 was the only airplane then available that had the speed and high-altitude performance to catch Japan's Ki-46 "Dinah" reconnaissance aircraft.

When the American Volunteer Group (AVG) began flying combat missions for China in late 1941, they inherited a handful of Chinese P-43s. These had been upgraded with some armor and fuel-tank protection and were mainly used in the photoreconnaissance and high-altitude interception roles. The Chinese did not have much success with the P-43 and when the AVG was reintegrated into the US Army Air Forces, (the USAAC became the USAAF in June 1941) as the 23rd Fighter Group, a handful of P-43s were transferred as well. These would be the only examples of the type to see combat under the American flag. Among those Americans qualified in the airplane was 1st Lt. William DiStefano of the group's 75th Fighter Squadron, who flew thirteen combat missions in the P-43 between April and June 1943, just prior to the type's final withdrawal from service in July of that year. It would be

Left: The P-43 Lancer did see combat in limited numbers in the China-Burma-India (CBI) Theater. In this theater the aircraft was mainly applied in the roles of high-altitude interceptor and reconnaissance aircraft.

The turbo was also the source of pressure for the ignition system."

The new airplane was massive. Even Alexander Kartveli was quoted in the October 5, 1942, edition of *Life* magazine, saying "It is too big!" in reference to the new fighter. The Thunderbolt, as it came to be known, was the largest and heaviest single-engine fighter ever made. Straight and level, it showed blistering speed and remarkable high-altitude performance. During testing at Wright Field on August 28, 1941, the XP-47B reached a top speed of 412mph (663kmh) at 25,800ft (7,864m), the first USAAC fighter to exceed 400mph (643kmh) in level flight.

The entire production run of P-47B aircraft lasted from May 1941 through September 1942, when the Farmingdale, New York, factory switched to C model production. The new C model replaced the P-47B's fabric-covered control surfaces with metal surfaces that were far more durable in the P-47's high-speed dive. In addition, after the first fifty-six C models were delivered, the P-47C-1 was introduced on the production line, which had a 13in (33cm) fuselage extension ahead of the wing leading edge. The P-47C-5 was the most numerous variant and was the first Thunderbolt to feature a centerline bomb rack. Combat experience in Europe quickly dictated that more range was critical, necessitating the centerline pylon to be plumbed for pressurized fuel lines, enabling the carriage of an external fuel tank.

nearly a year before the Lancer's younger brother would take to the skies over China.

Eight months after its contract was awarded, the prototype XP-47B was unveiled to USAAC brass. Two days later, on May 6, 1941, it took to the skies for the first time, with Republic chief test pilot Lowery Brabham at the controls. It delivered a satisfactory first flight, and the Air Corps ordered another 855 P-47Ds as a result. By the beginning of 1942, Republic had set up a second production line in Evansville, Indiana, and a third at Curtiss Aircraft in Buffalo, New York, but very few P-47Bs had been produced by the end of 1941 due to a number of issues with the design.

As Republic's chief test pilot, it fell on Brabham's shoulders not only to fly the aircraft, but to identify and solve problems the new type encountered. "First we ran into troubles with ignition, as the turbo supercharger gave such high internal cylinder pressures at the higher levels that sparking could not bring on ignition since at the lower density the spark jumped to some convenient spot outside the cylinder. This was finally solved by pressurizing the entire ignition system. A little higher the oil boiled to the point that all oil pressure could not be maintained. [The] Simple solution was bleeding pressure from the turbo into the oil tank.

In June, the first production P-47Bs reached the first unit to fly the Thunderbolt. The 56th Fighter Group's three squadrons rotated in flying the initial airframes, and as more became available they were issued out to the group's 61st, 62nd, and 63rd Fighter Squadrons. On receiving their aircraft, the 56th's squadrons moved from Mitchell Field, New York, to two airfields outside Hartford, Connecticut, where they established the training program for the new airplane and began putting it through its paces.

It was during this time in Connecticut that the 56th first encountered the Thunderbolt's phenomenal diving capability and the aerodynamic series airplanes, which debuted in the late fall of 1944, that a dive flap was installed under each wing to assist the pilot in dive speed control.

Although it was the first unit to fly the Thunderbolt, the 56th Fighter Group was not the first unit to take the P-47 into combat. The first P-47Cs arrived in England in March 1943, and the 4th Fighter Group, the famed "Eagle Squadrons," began transitioning from their small, sleek Spitfires into the massive Thunderbolt, which weighed more than twice that of their Spitfire Mk Vbs. The 4th was skeptical at best, but soon developed effective tactics that focused on the Thunderbolt's high-altitude performance and diving ability. Until that point, the standard German tactic to disengage was simply to dive away from a pursuer. Suddenly Luftwaffe pilots attempting to escape found themselves with seven tons of Thunderbolt firmly glued to their tail!

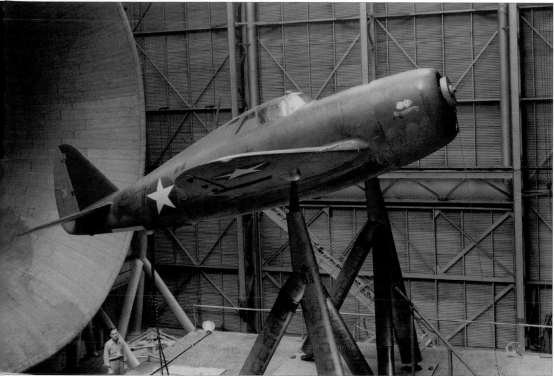

Above: A full-scale airplane was used in a wind tunnel to address control-surface issues in high-speed dives.
Right: The XP-47B prototype made its maiden flight on May 6, 1941, with Republic test pilot Lowery Brabham at the controls.

phenomena known as compressibility. When the P-47 entered a dive, its speed increased rapidly. As the airplane neared the speed of sound, the airflow on the leading edge of the wing would begin to compress. This compression disturbed the airflow over the wing and built up a supersonic shockwave that effectively separated the airflow from the wing surface. The airplane would still be sub-sonic, but the airflow around it would already be supersonic. The resulting airflow separation from the wing and airframe effectively ceased the airflow over the control surfaces on the airplane's tail, making it impossible to pull out of a dive until the airplane slowed and normal airflow over the control surfaces resumed.

The 56th Fighter Group had a number of fatal crashes in those first few months of P-47 operations, and they were eventually attributed to unrecoverable dives due to compressibility. Several piloting techniques were created to mitigate the effects, but it was not until the P-47D-30

It was also during the P-47's entry into combat that several nicknames arose. "Repulsive Scatterbolt" was one of the less-endearing terms, but the one that stuck was the "Jug," an abbreviation of Juggernaut. The P-47 was fast, hit hard, and could absorb massive amounts of damage and keep flying. It was an unstoppable juggernaut, and the name fit.

A month after the 4th introduced the Jug to combat, the 56th Fighter Group arrived in England as the second P-47 unit, and the 78th Fighter Group followed suit shortly thereafter. Back in the United States, the Republic factory in Farmingdale had upgraded the production line again, and in February began producing the P-47D with several internal improvements in the turbocharger, hydraulic, fuel, and electrical systems, plus increased armor protection for the pilot. The first Ds were externally identical to the P-47C-5, but the need for increased engine cooling necessitated more cowl flaps around the aft end of the cowling in order to improve airflow over the cylinders. The first Ds from the Republic Farmingdale factory would arrive in May and from Evansville in September. Farmingdale-produced airplanes would be identified by the two-letter manufacturer code RE, while Evansville airplanes would be coded RA.

As combat reports began to filter back about the Thunderbolt's performance, the Army began to suggest improvements to the manufacturer. The heavy framed canopy of the Jug was a source of some consternation, as it limited visibility to the sides and to the rear, as did the high back of the fuselage. Pilot visibility is the key to survival in fighter aircraft, and as a result Republic took a P-47D-10 off the production line, cut down the rear fuselage and added a modified clear plexiglass canopy from a British Hawker Typhoon. The resulting XP-47K was far superior to all previous models of the Thunderbolt when it came to pilot visibility; the tradeoff, however, was a reduction in lateral stability due to the loss of fuselage surface area. When the XP-47K test data was collected in the summer and fall of 1943, the modifications were planned for incorporation into the production line at both the Farmingdale and Evansville plants with the P-47D-25-RE (Farmingdale) and 26-RA (Evansville) production blocks.

The last two Thunderbolt variants to enter service both did so in early 1945. The P-47M was a true "hot rod." Based on the P-47D-30 airframe, the M had the new R2800C-57 engine and larger CH-5 supercharger in place of the D-30's R2800-63W engine. The powerplant put out 2,800hp and pushed the M to a whopping 480mph (772kmh) at 30,000ft (9,143m). Only 130 of these speed demons were built, and all were issued to the sole remaining 8th Air Force P-47 group, the 56th, starting in January 1945. Despite some initial setbacks, the P-47M proved a phenomenal airplane and a deadly weapon even against the new German jets.

Lastly, and developed concurrently with the M, was the P-47N. The N was the ultimate Thunderbolt to see combat and was the result of five years of constant refinement to Alexander Kartveli's original design. The P-47N had a completely redesigned wing that incorporated new self-sealing fuel tanks, extending the Jug's range to more than 2,000 miles (3,219km) on internal fuel and to nearly 3,000 miles (4,828km) with three external tanks. Yet it too was somewhat of a hot rod. The N topped out at roughly 470mph (756kmh) at 35,000ft (10,667m). It could carry 3,500lb (1,588kg) of ordnance for eight hours over vast expanses of the Pacific, in order to attack the Japanese home islands, which it did from May to August 1945.

Experimental models

The old fighter pilot adage that "speed is life" was clearly evident in Thunderbolt development. Combat pilots had already established the "boom and zoom" tactic of diving on an enemy fighter from high altitude, firing at it, and then using the airplane's energy to "zoom climb" back up to altitude before the enemy could react. The airplane was already fast straight and level, and was uncatchable in a dive. Yet Republic sought to make it even faster and experimented with several different designs and powerplants to squeeze every last ounce of speed out of the airframe.

One of the major airframe redesigns incorporated the massive 2,500hp Chrysler XIV-2220 liquid-cooled inverted-vee engine mated with P-47D-15-RA serial numbers 42-23297 and 23298. Delays in engine testing and production held back the program and the XP-47H's first flight did not occur until the war was nearly over, on July 26, 1945. Performance improved to 490mph (788kmh), but did not reach the targeted 500mph+ (805kmh+) that the USAAF sought.

Designated after the XP-47H, but developed before it, the XP-47J was the fastest example of the Thunderbolt family. The J-model was Republic's response to an Army Air Forces request for a lightweight P-47 built around the new R-2800C-57 engine and CH-5 supercharger. Alexander Kartveli redesigned the cowling to fit much closer around the engine and added a cooling fan and spinner around the prop hub, similar to the German Fw 190. In addition to the new powerplant, the XP-47J's wing was lightened and the main armament was reduced to six .50-caliber machine guns. The resulting airframe was only 400lb (182kg) lighter than the P-47D, but the refinements to the design paid off. On August 4, 1944, Republic test pilot Mike Ritchie flew the XP-47J on a closed course, reaching 505mph (813kmh) in level flight. Although the record-setting flight proved conventional propeller-driven fighters could break the 500mph (805kmh) mark, the decision was made not to put the type into full-scale production, as it would require retooling of more than 70 percent of the Republic production line when delays in production were not possible. Instead, the lessons learned allowed the powerplant and supercharger from the XP-47J to be directly installed in the P-47D-30-RE airframe, resulting in the P-47M, the fastest production Thunderbolt.

The last major test P-47 incorporated the new 3,450hp R-4360 "corn cob" engine and as a result was given a completely new designation, the XP-72. The original design called for two counter-rotating Aeroproducts

Right: A ground crew member fits fuses on 250lb (113kg) M57 and 500lb (227kg) M64 General Purpose bombs, while 75-gallon (284-liter) external fuel tanks (or napalm tanks) and crates of .50-caliber machine-gun ammunition wait to be loaded.

propellers, but delays with the gearing system on the propellers resulted in the first example, XP-72 43-36598, being completed with a standard four-bladed propeller. The first prototype flew with the conventional propeller on February 2, 1944, and the second flew with the Aeroproducts propellers on June 26. A crash on takeoff destroyed the second prototype, but the Army Air Forces was impressed with the XP-72's performance and ordered one hundred of the aircraft. Yet by late 1944, it was clear that jet-powered fighters were the future of fighter development. As a result, the 100 airplane contract was terminated by the end of the war, with only the two prototypes having been built.

While each of the experimental types provided Republic with more insight on the development potential of the Thunderbolt airframe, all three of them were designed as short-ranged interceptors rather than long-range escort fighters. This ensured that while the technology they developed could be incorporated into the P-47 blocks on the production line, the XP-47H, XP-47J and XP-72 would remain as technological marvels rather than as combat aircraft.

Engines and propellers

The Pratt & Whitney R2800 18-cylinder Double Wasp engine was the Thunderbolt's beating heart. Designed around the massive 2,000hp engine, the Jug became the largest and heaviest single-engine fighter adopted by the US military. While other fighters like the Navy's Hellcat and Corsair used variants of the R2800, neither had the Thunderbolt's complex supercharger ductwork, which directed the engine exhaust back to the supercharger under the aft fuselage.

The P-47 owes its high-altitude performance to the two-stage turbocharger. It gave early versions of the Thunderbolt their best performance at 27,000ft (8,230m), while later bubbletop variants saw their best performance at just above 30,000ft (9,143m). The supercharger works by exhaust gases blowing against a bucket wheel attached to the same shaft. The supercharged air is then forced into the intake via the intercoolers. The intercooler doors on the sides of the fuselage either direct the exhaust gases to the bucket wheel or allow them to escape, providing a few extra miles per hour's worth of thrust.

The P-47B, C, and early D models were equipped with the R2800-21 engine, which produced 2,000hp at maximum output. Beginning with the P-47D-5-RE, a 15-gal (57-liter) tank was added to the engine firewall; the tank held a solution of methanol and water for better cylinder cooling at high-power settings. Initially the water injection was manually controlled, but this system attracted negative pilot feedback; they criticized having to shift attention away from combat to make sure to engage the water injection for War Emergency Power. The system was subsequently made automatic on the P-47D-11-RE and engaged automatically when the throttle was roughly ⅛in (3mm) from full forward.

The R2800-21W with water injection boosted engine output by roughly 15 percent, increasing the total horsepower to 2,300hp in War Emergency Power. The initial 15-gal (57-liter) tank gave the pilot roughly 15 minutes of water injection. This was further modified on late-model Thunderbolts, which had nearly twice the capacity.

War Emergency Power could literally mean the difference between life and death in a dogfight. On numerous occasions, Thunderbolt pilots found themselves with an enemy fighter on their tail, and simply pushing

Above: *This top view of an early P-47B over Long Island, 1942, shows the overall profile of the aircraft to good effect, particularly the thick fuselage and the airplane's long, heavy nose.*

the throttle into War Emergency Power allowed them to outdistance their pursuers and disengage, living to fight another day. Conversely, the extra speed that War Emergency Power provided allowed many a P-47 pilot to accelerate to catch a fleeing enemy aircraft, which quickly met its fate on the receiving end of eight .50-caliber machine guns.

The R2800 guzzled gas. Normal cruise fuel consumption was between 90 and 130 gals (340 and 492 litres) per hour. However, once in combat and the throttle was advanced to full military power, the consumption rate would jump up to roughly 275 gals (1,040 liters) per hour and with War Emergency Power, it increased even further to a whopping 315 gals (1,192 liters) per hour.

Water injection helped the P-47 immensely, but the original 12ft (3.65m) diameter Curtiss Electric CE714-1C2-12 propeller was unable to provide the necessary thrust to make the Thunderbolt really perform. Nicknamed the "toothpick" because of its narrow blades, the Curtiss prop was the factory standard propeller from the P-47B through the P-47D-21-RE. Because the propeller lacked surface area to really "bite" into the air, the early model Thunderbolts climbed slowly. As combat reports came back to Republic criticizing the slow rate of climb, upgrades were planned and executed with all due haste. As a result, the P-47D-22-RE and -23-RA production blocks (Republic Farmingdale and Evansville respectively) introduced the 13ft (3.96m) Hamilton Standard 6501A-2 and Curtiss Electric (A.O. Smith) 836-2C2-18 broad chord propellers, mated to the R2800-59W or R2800-63W engines (rated at 2,600hp War Emergency Power), which greatly improved the Thunderbolt's anemic climb rate.

However, when the ultimate Thunderbolts finally entered combat service in early 1945, they utilized a completely new series of R2800. The P-47M and N used the new R2800 C series engines, the R2800-57 and R2800-77 respectively, which added an additional 500 horsepower at War Emergency Power, topping out at a full 2,800hp. The P-47M was the fastest-climbing variant, with a 3,900ft (1,188m) per minute initial rate of climb that was comparable to the twin-engine P-38J, and in fact under test conditions,

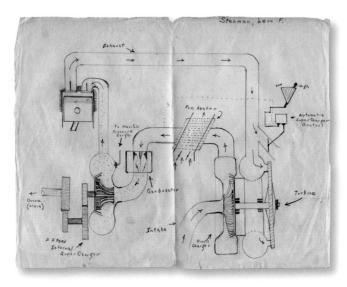

Left: SSgt. Leon Stehman's hand-drawn diagram of the Thunderbolt's supercharger, showing the flow of fuel, gases, and power around the system. The aircraft had their best performance at just above 30,000ft (9,143m), with the B, C, and early D models producing 2,000hp at maximum output.

the M could outclimb the P-38J to 20,000ft (6,095m). Both the P-47M and P-47N used the symmetric-bladed 836-14C2-1081, which gave the best overall performance.

While the R2800 was the largest, most powerful engine ever installed in an USAAF fighter, it was also the most survivable. No engine in the American inventory during World War II had the combat damage record established by the Double Wasp. The Thunderbolt had a reputation for absorbing massive amounts of damage, but its engine was even more durable. As noted, there have been numerous accounts of Thunderbolt pilots pulling up from a low-level strafing run and realizing their engine is "running a little rough," only to examine the engine upon return to base and find that an entire cylinder housing had simply been blown off by antiaircraft artillery (AAA) fire. The engine's ability to run with its oil supply coating the entire airframe (and often the pilot!) was well documented, and many a Thunderbolt pilot brought his wounded bird home by rolling back the canopy and looking out the side to line up for a perfect three-point landing.

Above: "Zombie" was a trainer P-47D-2-RE assigned to Perry Army Airfield, Florida. At Perry, pilots received their final training in P-40 Warhawks, P-47 Thunderbolts, and P-51 Mustangs.

Combat History

The P-47 was designed during a time when long range was not considered essential to combat performance. Yet the realities of World War II combat forced the Thunderbolt to evolve. As an escort fighter, the "Jug" was an adequate bomber escort for the shorter-range missions to targets in France. However, by the fall of 1943, with the strategic bombing campaign's focus on German war industry, many targets were simply too far away for the P-47 to provide effective escort for the bombers.

The two greatest criticisms of the Jug were its slow rate of climb and its lack of range. External fuel tanks were the simplest answer to the range issue, and improvements to the size and number of tanks available increased through the summer of 1943, leading up to the Emden raid on September 27, 1943. This raid was the first of many missions in which 8th Air Force Thunderbolts were able to escort B-17 and B-24 bombers all the way to Germany, engage the Luftwaffe (and shoot down twenty-two enemy airplanes for only one loss), and return with the bombers. Yet as the year went on, bombing raids ventured ever farther into Germany, where the Jug's range would not allow it to follow.

Range was a key reason the Thunderbolt was slow to appear in the Pacific as well. The 348th Fighter Group arrived in Australia in the late spring 1943, and went into combat over New Guinea in August of that year. The 348th, under the charismatic leadership of Col. Neel Kearby, quickly changed the 5th Air Force commanding general's opinion of the Thunderbolt, by asserting air superiority over Lae and Nadzab. Using the Thunderbolt's speed and high-altitude performance, they quickly began racking up large numbers of kills against some of the best pilots in the Japanese military. As a result, more units in the Pacific and in the China-Burma-India (CBI) Theater began to convert to the P-47 late in the year.

In all, nine groups flew the Thunderbolt in the Pacific theater, although not all saw combat. Both the 15th and 318th Fighter Groups flew defensive combat air patrols from Hawaii in early 1944. While the 318th went on to establish a significant combat record in both the P-47D and P-47N between June 1944 and August 1945, the 15th turned in their Razorback P-47D-21s and transitioned to Very Long Range (VLR) navigation-equipped P-51Ds for the final campaign against the Japanese home islands.

Above: *The M6 Bomb Service Truck and M5 Bomb Trailer were used to bring ordnance from the squadron bomb dump to the flightline. Handling the truck and trailer were jobs requiring both strong nerves and skilled driving.*

The majority of the Pacific Theater Thunderbolts fought in the skies over New Guinea and the Philippines, performing equally well against Japanese aircraft and ground targets. The 35th Fighter Group was one of the first US fighter units to engage the Japanese, albeit with the mediocre P-39 Airacobra or its export equivalent, the P-400. The 35th gave up its Airacobras and its handful of P-38 Lightnings in the fall of 1943 and completed the transition to the Thunderbolt by year's end, following the 348th Fighter Group, which had proven the Thunderbolt's effectiveness in a theater where most thought it would fail as a fighter. The 35th, 58th, and 348th Fighter Groups, along with 5th Air Force P-38s, virtually cleared the skies of Japanese aircraft during 1944–45 and maintained air superiority over the Philippines until war's end. While the 58th and 348th continued combat operations in the P-47 throughout the remainder of the war, the 35th Fighter Group traded in their trusty Thunderbolts in March 1945 in favor of P-51Ds and a change of mission to the bomber escort role.

Meanwhile, as the air forces shuffled around responsibilities in Europe and the Mediterranean, it was decided that the 12th Air Force would become the tactical air force in the Mediterranean and its fighter units would re-equip entirely with the P-47. Ultimately the 12th was responsible for six P-47 groups, starting with the 57th, which re-entered combat in October 1943 after transitioning from the P-40F.

By late spring 1944, the P-47's mediocre rate of climb was finally addressed by adopting a broader chord propeller that better used engine power and got a better "bite" into the air (see above). By December 1943, the 56th started refitting their older airplanes and began acquiring new P-47D-22-RE and D-23-RA aircraft with more powerful engines and the new Hamilton and Curtiss propellers. The increase in rate of climb would now allow the Jug to outclimb an Fw 190 below 15,000ft (4,572m).

The Thunderbolt could carry the largest bomb load of any single-engine fighter that saw service during World War II. Its primary armament was a battery of eight .50-caliber AN/M2 aircraft machine guns, each capable of firing 850 rounds per minute (rpm). Each gun was fed by a belt of 475 rounds laid in the ammunition troughs inside the wing. Several types of rounds were available, but most often used were standard M2 ball, M8 armor-piercing incendiary, M10 tracer, and, by the end of the war, the even harder-hitting T48 armor-piercing incendiary round, which was standardized as the M23 API. It was conventional practice to load the last fifty rounds of each belt of .50-caliber ammunition with tracer rounds, so that the pilot would have a visual cue letting him know that he was about to run out of ammunition.

The P-47 carried a useful bomb load of 2,500lb (1,134kg), although under certain conditions heavier loads could be and were carried. The most commonly carried bomb type

Left and below: .50-caliber M2 ball ammunition. P-47s at operational and replacement training units usually only flew with two guns per wing.

was the AN/M64 500lb (227kg) General Purpose (GP) bomb. The high-explosive filler was roughly 200lb (91kg) of a 50/50 mix of Amatol and TNT, the remaining weight being made up by the bomb's steel casing.

GP bombs were a compromise between high-explosive and fragmentation types, and were therefore usable against a wider range of targets. Fragmentation bombs used the bomb's explosion to saturate an area with shrapnel, primarily aimed at killing personnel and destroying unarmored equipment. The 260lb (118kg) AN/M81 fragmentation bomb was the principal type of fragmentation weapon used until the 20lb (9kg) AN/M41 fragmentation cluster bomb was adopted. These bombs would be packaged on a common bomb shackle, usually between six and eighteen bombs on a single rack, and were used extensively against personnel and soft targets in support of friendly troops on the ground.

Thunderbolts of the 57th Fighter Group were the first unit to use napalm in combat during the summer of 1944, and the weapon's usefulness against stubborn resistance was undeniable. The Naphthalene Palmitate gelling agent, mixed with gasoline and loaded into a standard 75-, 110-, or 165-gal (284-, 416-, or 165-liter) drop tanks became a devastating fire bomb that was effective against tanks, fixed targets, and urban areas.

The last weapon in the Thunderbolt's arsenal was the aerial rocket. P-47-mounted rockets came in two forms, the 4.5in (114mm) fin-stabilized "bazooka" rockets, mounted in triple tubes under each wing, or the later 5in (127mm) High Velocity Aircraft Rockets (HVAR) mounted on zero-length rocket stubs under the wing. Initial combat use of the bazooka rockets was relatively unfavorable, as precision was lacking and the rockets tended to go where they wanted, not where the pilot was aiming. Yet as techniques improved, both types of rocket became devastating weapons, both against ground targets and, in the case of Capt. Judge Wolfe's confirmed kill on a Japanese Ki-84 "Frank," against airborne targets as well!

With the multitude of weapon systems at the Jug pilot's fingertips, how did he put ordnance on target? During its combat history, the Thunderbolt used three primary sighting systems, each usually backed up by the old-fashioned ring and bead sights. The first illuminated gunsight mounted on the P-47 was the N-3B, which was the standard early World War II fighter gunsight. The sight projected an illuminated reticle on an angled piece of glass in the pilot's line of sight. He could then use the concentric rings of the reticle to estimate target lead and deflection angle before opening fire. The second type of sight was a modification of the

British Mk 8 gunsight, which had a larger field of view and was mounted closer to the pilot, allowing better eye relief. This type was common on the majority of Thunderbolts produced in 1944. The final type was introduced on the P-47D-28-RE and was on all subsequent models of the Jug. The K-14 gyro-stabilized computing gunsight was a remarkable piece of technology that allowed the pilot to dial in the wingspan of his intended target; the gunsight would then compute the lead angle and give the pilot an accurate firing solution.

The tactical and technological evolutions of the P-47 were reflected in its training manuals. The late-1944 pilot-training manual had the benefit of experience behind it. Modifications, upgrades, and nearly two years of combat experience had made the manual's opening quote a reality: "The P-47 is a jack-of-all-trades, and, contrary to tradition, a master of all. The plane was designed originally as a high altitude fighter, but the exigencies of war brought it downstairs. The Thunderbolt now does dive bombing, skip bombing, strafing and rocket launching as well as high altitude escort. It does them all superbly well. Terrific firepower keeps the enemy ducking, and the plane's heavy construction withstands savage punishment. Plenty of pilots in the ETO call the P-47 the best fighter in the world for low-altitude work."

Pilot training

One of the best advantages Thunderbolt pilots had over the enemy was their training. A Thunderbolt pilot would normally enter the Operational Training phase of flight training with an average of 235 hours of flight training through Primary (60 hours), Basic (75 hours), Advanced (70 hours), and Fighter Transition (30 hours) phases.

By the fall of 1944, aviation cadets attended a ten-week preflight training course at the San Antonio Aviation Cadet Center. This was the cadet's basic military indoctrination course. It focused on military life and physical training and included about five hours of daily academic training. Once this was completed, the cadet would move on to Primary Flight Training and would start flying, usually in a Stearman PT-17 Kaydet biplane. This phase would teach basic flight maneuvers and piloting skills. Graduation led the student pilot on to Basic Flight Training for the next few months, where he would learn the principles of instrument flight and formation flying in a more complex airplane, the all-metal Vultee BT-

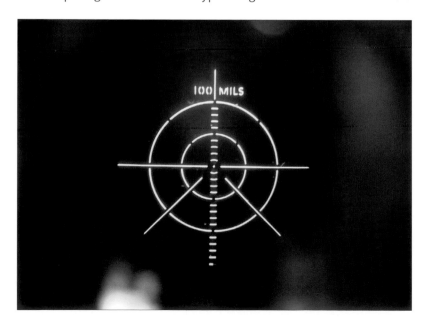

100 MILS

Above: *The illuminated target reticle projected on the P-47's Mark 8 gunsight. The system had the virtue that it was easier for the pilot to keep the reticle on the target even when being jostled around in the cockpit.*

13/15 Valiant (affectionately known by pilots as the Vultee Vibrator). The Advanced phase introduced the student pilot to a complex aircraft in form of the T-6 Texan. The T-6 would be the pilots' first experience with retractable landing gear and it would also initiate them into aerobatic maneuvers and basic gunnery.

When a student pilot completed all three phases and was set on the fighter pilot track, he was then sent on to Fighter Transition, where he would learn to fly fighters on obsolete types like the P-40. This would be their first exposure to high-performance aircraft, combat flight maneuvers, and fighter gunnery, both against ground targets and against the air-to-air RP-63 "pinball," a specially modified P-63 Kingcobra designed to take hits from frangible .50-caliber ammunition fired from the student's airplane. Finally designated a "fighter pilot" after thirty hours of instruction, the student would then begin a five-week transition at an Operational Training Unit on the type he would fly in combat.

The training pipeline normally took an Aviation Cadet approximately fifty-two weeks to graduate as a Thunderbolt pilot and get posted to an operational unit. With another seventy hours in the cockpit before reaching his unit, a Thunderbolt pilot's training allowed him to be comfortable in his aircraft, know its idiosyncrasies and its strengths. He had just enough knowledge to get himself killed if he wasn't careful. A pilot was not ready for combat until a year or more after he started flying instruction.

Once a Thunderbolt pilot was shipped overseas, his training was not yet complete. Arriving in theater, a new pilot would then be posted to a Fighter Training Group (FTG), like the 495th FTG in England. The 495th was responsible for the final training phase for all new Thunderbolt pilots and acquainted the fledgling aviators with the peculiarities of flying in Europe, the capabilities of enemy aircraft, and what to expect when posted to a unit. The 495th trained P-47 pilots from May 1943 through the end of the war, providing new blood for both the 8th and 9th Air Forces during that time.

When finally assigned to a squadron, new pilots would be given a local area orientation flight, flying as wingman for one of the more senior pilots in the squadron, if not the group. When signed off to start flying missions, pilots could expect to fly roughly every other day. The twenty-six airplanes assigned to a squadron were rarely all combat-ready at once, and routine maintenance schedules assured that a third of the squadron's airplanes were usually having some form of work done at any given time. This allowed for the rotation of both pilots and airplanes, making them far more combat effective, while their Japanese and German opponents flew on a daily basis (often more than one mission a day) until either they were wounded, killed, or the war ended.

With his training complete, the new Thunderbolt pilot was ready for his first combat mission. . . .

Composition of a Fighter Squadron

The USAAF Fighter Squadron, (Single Engine) Table of Organization and Equipment (TO&E) underwent several changes during the course of World War II. As changes resulting from lessons learned were put into operational practice, the TO&E was finalized by December 1944. The primary assets of a fighter squadron were the twenty-five single-engine fighters assigned. Regardless of fighter type, the squadron had the same basic structure, with only minor modifications to accommodate mission-specific equipment. Each squadron included a flight echelon and ground echelon, which clearly defined mission tasks for assigned personnel. The flight echelon included all pilots, ground crews, and operations personnel, totaling 121 officers and enlisted men. The ground echelon (164 officers and enlisted men) included all heavy maintenance, supply, intelligence, and mess sections, along with all of the squadron's twenty-six assigned ground vehicles. The two halves worked seamlessly together toward a common mission, but were occasionally separated when the squadron moved to a new airfield. This was particularly the case in the Pacific, while the air echelon would fly to a new location, leaving the ground element to arrive several days later by ship. USAAF fighter groups each had at least three fighter squadrons assigned (occasionally four) and usually flew from the same airfield during combat operations, although squadrons could have some degree of autonomy.

Above: This grainy image depicts a flight of trainer P-47s from a stateside Replacement Training Unit.

Aircraft Walkaround

Above: *Although it does not depict a specific 84th Fighter Squadron airplane, P-47D-40-RA 45-49385 clearly shows what the last Jugs assigned to the 78th Fighter Group looked like before they transitioned to the Mustang in December 1944.*

Right: *BREAK!—45-49385 and 45-49346 perform a formation break for the camera ship. Both airplanes were delivered to the USAAF in summer 1945 and served as stateside trainers before being sold to South American air forces in the early 1950s.*

Left: *P-47 45-49346 clearly shows the bubbletop Thunderbolt's advantage in pilot visibility.*

Right: *The only flying Thunderbolt representing the P-47M, this airplane was delivered as a P-47D-40-RA but wears accurate colors for the 63rd Fighter Squadron in the closing months of the war.*

Below: *Visual recognition bands, painted on the wings and fuselage, were added in preparation for the D-Day invasion on June 6, 1944.*

Opposite page top left: *Jeff Clyman's "Jacky's Revenge" represents the 353rd Fighter Group's P-47 period, although the 353rd never received P-47D-40s for P-47 ops.*

Opposite page lower left: *Claire Aviation Co.'s Thunderbolt flies in the personal markings of 82nd Fighter Squadron pilot Lt. Benjamin Mayo, Jr., "No Guts, No Glory."*

Right: *One of only two flying "Razorback" P-47s, this Curtiss-built P-47G currently flies in the markings of Maj. Walker "Bud" Mahurin's P-47D-5 "Spirit of Atlantic City New Jersey."*

Below left: *Identification lights under the right wingtip helped ground personnel and other aircraft to identify friendly aircraft from enemy. Each light could be turned on independently and could be set to blink or remain steady as the day's IFF orders dictated.*

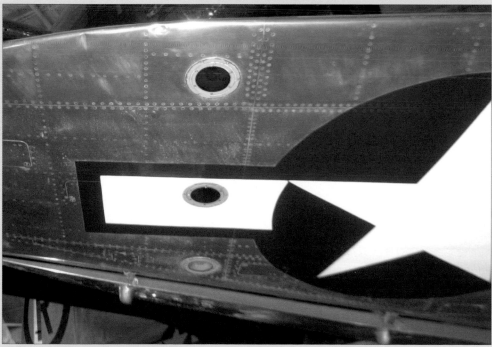

Right: *The beating heart of the P-47 was the massive Pratt & Whitney R2800-63W Double Wasp turning a 13ft (4m) Curtiss Electric (shown here) or Hamilton Standard propeller.*

Right: *All Army Air Forces aircraft had a similar data block indicating the project number, aircraft block and serial numbers, crew weight, and general servicing instructions.*

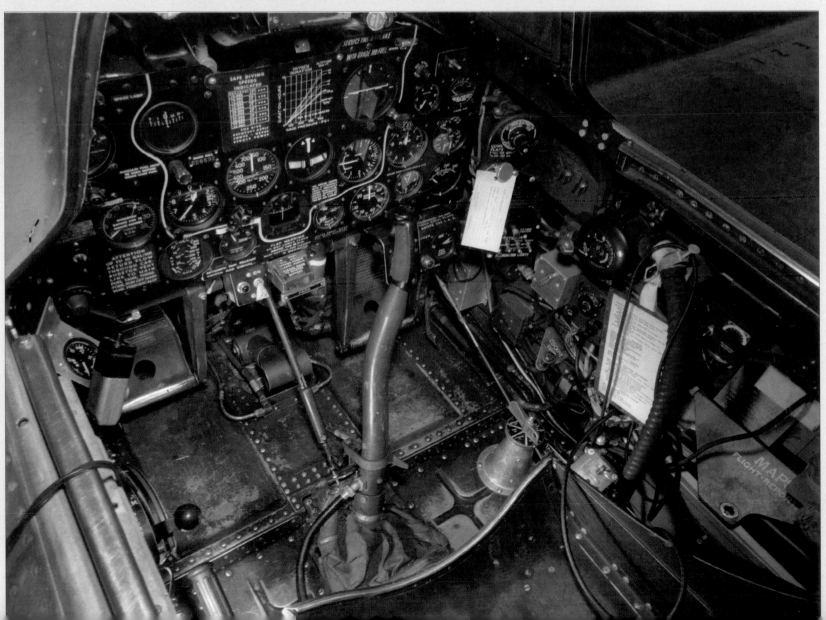

A.A.F. PROJECT NO. 24579-34
U.S. ARMY MODEL P-47D-40-RA
A.A.F. SERIAL NO. 45-49385

CREW WEIGHT 200 LBS.
SERVICE THIS AIRPLANE WITH GRADE
100/130 FUEL. IF NOT AVAILABLE T.O
06-03-1 WILL BE CONSULTED FOR
EMERGENCY ACTION
SUITABLE FOR AROMATICS

Opposite page, right: *The elevators, which control climb and descent, are connected by a rod that passes through the airplane's rudder.*

Opposite page, far right: *The "kicker arm" on the back of the Thunderbolt's wing pylons ensured the clean separation of bombs or fuel tanks during a dive-bombing run.*

Opposite page, below: *Each wing contained four .50-caliber AN/M2 machine guns, each with 475 rounds of belted ammunition.*

Below: *The "office," in this case the cockpit of P-47D-25-RE 42-26592.*

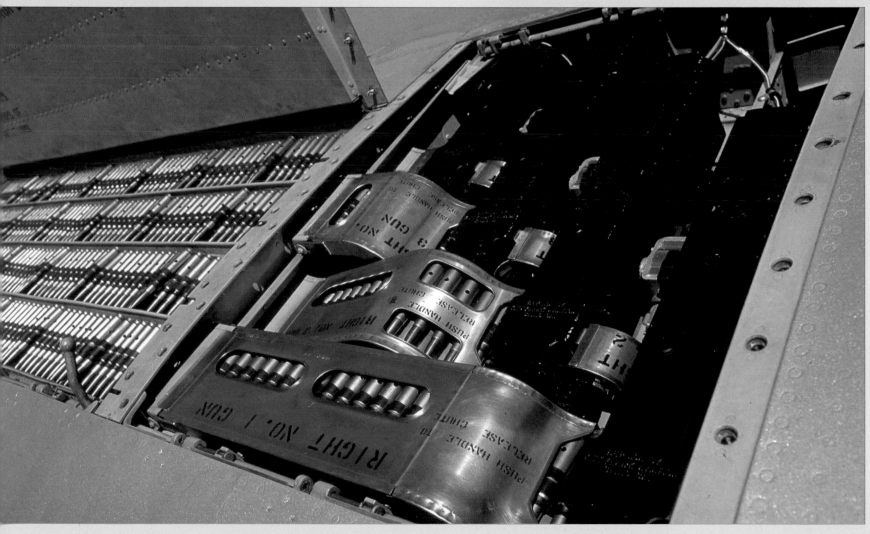

Above left: *The Thunderbolt's retractable main gear tucked neatly within the airplane's wing inboard of the pylons and wing machine guns.*

Above right: *Inside a P-47N fuselage looking forward—the two large square ducts lead to the intercooler doors on the fuselage sides, while the circular duct is the exhaust duct leading back to the CH-5 supercharger.*

Left: *The fin fillet was retrofitted to many earlier bubbletop P-47s, but was standardized on the production line in the D-28 blocks. It returned a great deal of lateral stability that was lost with the addition of the bubble canopy.*

Right: *With the introduction of the Hamilton Standard 6501 propeller in the late spring 1944, the Thunderbolt's climb performance was significantly upgraded. The propeller was very easy on maintenance and as a result is what equips most current flying Thunderbolts.*

PART 2

The Missions

Preparation for a Mission

Thunderbolt mission planning and preparation evolved just like the airplanes that flew the missions. When P-47s began flying combat in the spring of 1943, their primary role was that of an escort fighter. As a result, mission planning was tied very closely to the big picture—where were the bombers headed? Mission priorities for bombing missions were dictated by HQ, US Strategic and Tactical Air Forces (USSTAF), according to the command's current strategic focus, whether it be the aircraft or petroleum industries or axis transportation infrastructure.

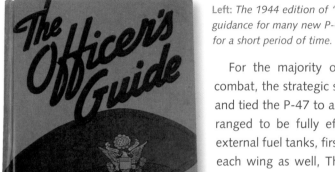

Left: The 1944 edition of "The Officer's Guide" provided guidance for many new P-47 pilots who had only been in uniform for a short period of time.

For the majority of the Thunderbolt's first year in combat, the strategic situation dictated mission planning and tied the P-47 to a mission in which it was too short-ranged to be fully effective. With the introduction of external fuel tanks, first on the centerline and then under each wing as well, Thunderbolts could escort bombers significantly farther into Axis-held territory, provided they weren't forced to drop their tanks and engage enemy fighters.

With the success of the Normandy invasion in June 1944, the Thunderbolt became the frontline fighter-bomber over Europe, while the number of P-51 Mustangs providing bomber escort increased. As 8th Air Force fighter groups converted to the Mustang, their Thunderbolts were passed to the 9th Air Force. During the summer of 1944, Thunderbolt unit mission briefings began to change. The P-47s were occasionally still called upon to provide bomber escort for 9th Air Force B-26s, and these did require a similar level of planning and detail as the 8th's missions of the previous year. But the most common P-47 missions flown in France, Belgium, Luxembourg, and Germany were armed reconnaissance and dive-bombing.

Planning for an armed reconnaissance mission was far simpler than the multi-layered process for escort missions, but each piece of the mission plan was no less critical. An armed reconnaissance mission is supposed to go out and look for the enemy, engage targets of opportunity, and return with critical information on troop dispositions, vehicles, aircraft, and other pertinent information. Planning for such a mission outlined radio frequencies, potential enemy units of interest, and a defined area to recon. The overall intelligence picture of the battlefield was critical as well. Where are the friendly troops? Where are the enemy troops and how far apart are the two sides? How are friendly troops marking their positions? The answers to these questions would be crucial to the success of an armed reconnaissance mission over enemy lines.

Above: Early P-47 Thunderbolts in their natural environment—sat at 25,000ft (7,620m) and above, providing fighter escort for B-17 and B-24 bombers on their way to attack the Axis.

As the squadron operations officer, Maj. Robert Hemphill of the 465th Fighter Squadron was responsible for not only flying on the actual missions, but planning them and issuing the mission roster:

"Tension begins when the operations officer walks in from his jeep and posts the proposed schedule for tomorrow's mission. You can feel it spread through camp like ink splashed on a blotter—but of course, nobody ever mentions it. You're coming back from mess or walking by the bulletin board in search of a guy with an uneducated deck of cards, when a cluster of pilots around the schedule brings you up short; wonder if I'm on tomorrow's show? And there's your name.

"Don't let anybody kid you, there is tension. It's not fear or wide-eyed unsureness. No one looks at the list, steps back panting and cries in a cracked voice 'My god, I can't do it again!'

Your bunch hasn't been in combat long enough, give them time. Maybe screaming meemies will get to be the regular thing. The tension you experience now is more like the kind you used to know trying to meet a deadline for publication or sitting in a white, antiseptic hospital waiting room while your wife went into the valley to give you a son, or one of your college profs to distribute his final examination.

Above: The 352nd Fighter Squadron's ready room provided a space for the crew to engage in critical mission preparation, with reference materials, maps, and the day's mission roster.

Right: More for off-duty use, but the US Army issue prophylactic kit was a critical piece of issued gear.

This tension is really your being aware that there is a job coming off, and that it's got to come off well or there'll be hell to pay. Such tension doesn't really hamper you; you feel it's a key winding up the mainspring of your system. By takeoff time tomorrow, you'll be a tiger waiting to get at the little bastards.

"Briefing is not like the movies say it is, the cheaters. No smoothly but casually dressed officer strides up to the covered map board, swagger stick in hand, presses a hidden button to reveal the map marked with route to target and announces dramatically, 'Gentlemen, today we visit McFiddlesburg on the Puntformation!'

"Instead an officer in crumpled khakis reads in a tired voice a typewritten field order telling the old basic newswriting answers to the who, what, when, where, and why. Other officers in crumpled khaki—some with red-rimmed eyes if they've been up all night compiling the

Once enemy forces were encountered, subsequent missions would be able to launch quickly with a hasty briefing of the mission, flak encountered by size and intensity, and any critical information deemed necessary for mission completion. Thunderbolt units operated close enough to the frontlines that one flight could be attacking the target, while another was headed back to refuel and rearm, and a third was en route to the target. The information gleaned from that first reconnaissance flight, which located the enemy force, would also dictate what ordnance the subsequent waves of Thunderbolts would carry. For example, fragmentation cluster bombs would be devastating against troops in the open, but only marginally effective against armored vehicles.

Interestingly, mission briefings for the late-war Very Long Range (VLR) fighter missions over the Japanese home islands were very similar in structure to those early 8th Air Force escort missions over Europe in 1943.

Above: Maj. Gen. William Kepner (third from left) was the consummate fighter leader and assumed command of the 8th Fighter Command in September 1943. Here he listens attentively to a mission briefing.

information you are now hearing—cover the points in more detail. By the time you get up from the rude seats and file out, you've made many notes on your kneeboard, information ranging from axis of attack to start-engine time."

For long-range missions, whether in April 1943 as bomber escorts or in July 1945 as long-range strike missions, Thunderbolt mission planners required a great deal of information to design an eight-hour mission successfully and bring back aircrews alive. Locations of enemy airfields and antiaircraft batteries were critical pieces of information; Knowing the potential threats greatly increased the Thunderbolt pilot's survivability. Arriving over an enemy airfield at 25,000ft (7,620m) rather than 20,000ft (6,096m) could mean the difference between life and death.

When the Thunderbolt's primary role shifted from escort to close support and interdiction, mission briefings changed drastically. While the 8th and 15th in the European Theater of Operations (ETO) and Mediterranean Theater of Operations (MTO) and the 7th in the Pacific flew one mission in eight hours, the 5th in the Pacific, 10th and 14th in the China-Burma-India (CBI) theater, and the 9th and 12th in Europe may have flown as many as six missions in the same eight-hour period. If ground units were in desperate need of air support, it was the Thunderbolt that was on-call. In the CBI Theater, during the battle for Myitkyina, 80th Fighter Group Thunderbolts were taking off, turning toward the target, dropping their bombs and strafing, and returning to load up with more bombs. Mission duration was roughly fifteen minutes, and they flew a lot of missions during that time.

The task of the operations officer, or S-3, was complicated by the fact that while his prime concern was to lead a mission and inflict the maximum damage on the enemy, and take an active part in the close-up tactical planning of every mission, he also had to supervise the endless paperwork connected with keeping the records and statistics. While other pilots logged a little sack time between missions, the ops officer performed his ground chores.

Conversely, the intelligence officer (S-2) was more than likely not a flying officer. The S-2 and S-3 put their heads together, poring over the information available in order to give their pilots the best picture possible about what lay ahead on tomorrow's mission. The intel officer had to be up on enemy units, movements, and intentions, almost on a minute-by-minute basis, or at least be able to give it his best guess! However, when the operations officer was flying the mission, the intel officer was busy gathering information in preparation for the next mission. He would debrief the pilots once they returned and incorporate any pertinent information into the following day's mission brief.

When it came to combat missions, relatively few hours were spent in the air when compared to the massive amount of intelligence gathering, aircraft and weapons maintenance, ordnance preparation, and finally mission planning. The 492nd Fighter Squadron ops officer put it succinctly: "Twenty four hours of every day are spent in planning, doing, and 'sweating it out.' If the scenes of an operational day's missions were presented kaleidoscopically, one would see a sleepy intelligence officer in the Group Ops trailer slooking down disconsolately at a clattering, inexorable teletype machine, nerve from the brain of the air force. The Intelligence Officer tears a jumble of terse words from the machine, consults target dossiers, draws lines on a map of western Europe, gets pin points, rouses his tired mind for rapid calculations.

"He calls squadron operations duty NCOs and states concisely: '108-gallon [409-liter] belly tank, two 1,000lb [454kg] bombs, ⅒ nose and .025 tail fusing, group briefing at 0630.' The Duty NCO phones a haggard CQ and later this CO and Operations Officer. The machine is now in low gear. The CQ begins his trips to the barracks to awaken the men. First are the cooks and KPs. Later he calls section heads and ground crews. Trucks stream from the motor pool to the barracks, sometimes to the mess hall, to the flightline. Soon pre-flighting begins and the engines cough and roar. Myriad red and blue navigational lights appear and seem to dance in the darkness. Engineering, Ordnance, Armament, and Communications men scurry about. There is a creaking of winches and bombs as the bombs are lifted to wing racks. Gas trucks hurry from plane to plane.

"Soon, drowsy pilots detruck at the briefing tent. They listen, now wideyeyed to 'Yardstick.' Then they make personal preparations. They go to the Snack Bar. Some go to the small house, but not in panic. The High Command may scrub the mission about this time. Otherwise the planes with enthusiastic crew chiefs riding the wings, trundle off to funnels at runway's end. An impersonal flier with a checkered flag waves them off by ones and twos, and they circle the field and form. The ground crews sigh, relax, but prepare for the next mission, consider wistfully the prospects of bad weather release, and wait.

"'Sir? Sir, wake up. You're on the schedule for today.'

Above: *Although the majority of fighter units were converting to the P-51 by the time Gen. Kepner left 8th Fighter Command, he retained his personal P-47, named "Kokomo," throughout the remainder of the war.*

Left: *The most common air-to-ground weapon employed by the P-47 was the AN/M64 500lb (227kg) General Purpose bomb.*

"You open your eyes slowly in the pre-dawn darkness and robotically pivot out of your cot, sliding your fleece-lined boots onto your feet, and grabbing your alpaca-lined flight jacket. You shiver as you head for the door. It's getting pretty cold in the mornings now as summer fades away. You've been living in a tent since Normandy and the rumor mill has it that the next airfield the squadron is moving and will have barracks buildings and hot running water.

"The mess tent is packed with other pilots and ground crews getting their morning issue of powdered eggs, chipped beef on toast (aka 'shit on a shingle'), and army coffee. The coffee hits the spot, making the food slightly more palatable, warming your insides and perking you up. You quickly finish your breakfast and head back to your bunk to grab your kneeboard, pencil, and flight computer.

"The mission brief is at 0630hrs, so you light a cigarette and wait outside the briefing tent until ten minutes before the scheduled start time. More of your squadron mates do the same as the nervous energy starts to build. You move along with everyone else as they file into the tent and take their seats.

"'Good morning gentlemen' the squadron intelligence officer begins. 'We've had reports of enemy armor massing near this crossroads, but so far have not been able to confirm that. Your job today is to find out what's there and if you find them, kill them. We need to know what's out there.'

"The Squadron Ops officer, your flight leader for today steps up next: 'Blue Flight will fly lead this mission, followed by Red Flight, with Yellow Flight providing top cover. Loads will be two M64 500-pounders and centerline tanks for Red and Blue Flight, just tanks for Yellow Flight. Engine start time is 0730hrs, so we're on a compressed timeline. We'll take off by flights, starting with Yellow Flight so they can gain a little altitude on us and then we will form up Red and Blue Flights over the field and turn east. I'll check in with our ground controller once we're formed up and get any last-minute instructions from him. Red Flight leader is the backup mission commander should something go wrong. We've got one spare for this mission, should someone have to abort due to mechanical issues. I don't anticipate we'll need it. Good luck, gentlemen—dismissed.'

"As you head outside the tent, there are three jeeps waiting to take you and the other twelve pilots out to the dispersal area and your aircraft. The ride only takes a few minutes and as you hop off the still-moving jeep, you see your ground crew already pulling the Thunderbolt's massive thirteen-foot propeller through several rotations.

Right: Communication was critical when conducting fighter operations. Army Air Forces fighter control squadrons were an essential part of the piece of the USAAF team.

Left: The Distinguished Flying Cross almost became a badge of office for Thunderbolt pilots.

Your crew chief gives you the rundown on what's loaded on the airplane. 'Sir, you've got a full load of .50-cal with the last fifty rounds of each belt as tracer, so you'll know when you're about to run out of ammo.'

"As you climb into the cockpit, he's already draping the shoulder harness over your shoulders and helping buckle you in. Hearing the click of the aluminum buckle, he signals to the other ground crew to step away from the prop arc.

"You run through your checklist quickly but thoroughly:

"Fuel selector to 'Main,' throttle cracked 1 inch [25mm], supercharger control—full aft. Mixture control is in 'Idle cut-off' and the propeller switch is on 'Automatic' with the circuit breaker in the on position. Propeller governor control should be full forward and your fuel boost pump should be in 'START and ALTITUDE.' You glance down at your watch: it's 0729hrs. One minute to engine start.

Above: These P-47s have just arrived in North Africa and would be quickly reassembled, test flown, and issued to the 57th and 325th Fighter Groups.

"Grabbing the primer handle, you prime four strokes, since it's a tad chilly out and then check the primer is locked in the off position. Flipping the Master Battery switch to 'ON,' you yell out 'CLEAR PROP!' and you hear echoes of the same down the flightline almost in unison. Ignition switch goes to 'BOTH' and starter switch to 'ENGAGE' and then immediately back to off in order to properly seat the starter brushes on the commutator.

"Moving the switch to 'ENERGIZE,' you hold it for another ten seconds and then switch it to 'ENGAGE' and the massive R2800 coughs, sputters, belches blue flame and smoke, and roars to life in unison with the rest of the squadron. You're ready."

Protect the Bombers!

"When they saw us coming, they rolled over and went in different directions but kept their altitude. One, the leader, pulled to the left and started climbing. Capt. Johnson, my leader, had begun to turn left after him. Capt. Johnson let a burst go and the Me 109 immediately broke right and spun. I was in a good position then and fired at him in the slow spin."

—1st Lt. Robert S. Johnson, 61st Fighter Squadron

The Thunderbolt's introduction to combat was somewhat lackluster. The redesignated 4th Fighter Group (previously 71, 121, and 133 Squadrons, RAF) had been integrated into the new 8th Air Force upon its arrival in England in the fall of 1942, and for those first few months the 4th continued flying their beloved Spitfire Vs, albeit now with US markings and codes.

In January 1943, however, the group began receiving the USAAF's latest fighter, the P-47C. Initial impressions were not favorable. The enormous P-47's takeoff weight was over twice that of the nimble Spitfire, something that unnerved the combat-experienced pilots of the 4th. They trained on the P-47 throughout the early months of 1943, and by early April the 334th, 335th, and 336th Fighter Squadrons were certified for combat.

Although quick to point out the Thunderbolt's weaknesses, the pilots of the 4th Fighter Group quickly learned about its strengths and capitalized on them. While it was slow to climb, the Thunderbolt had an incredible ability to dive and an astonishing rate of roll. Allied pilots who had fought the Germans were often frustrated by the German tactic of diving away to disengage, since the Spitfire had difficulty following the Me 109 or the Fw 190. Now they had an airplane that not only could catch the

Left: The P-47C 41-6243, flown by the 84th Fighter Squadron's Capt. George Hays, keeps close as it escorts an 8th Air Force B-17 Flying Fortress home.

enemy when he tried to dive away, but had more than enough firepower to destroy him once they did.

The 334th Squadron's monthly history entry on February 28, 1943, echoes the mixed emotions about the new airplane: "Although sorry to say farewell to the Spitfires which had carried them over enemy territory so often, and although they naturally disliked changing from known to new aircraft, our pilots were hopeful that the new Thunderbolts would give them an even better weapon. . . ."

Ten days later, the 334th Fighter Squadron was the first to take the Thunderbolt over enemy territory, on March 10. Launching at 1515hrs, the formation of eleven P-47Cs, led by Col. Chesley Peterson, crossed the Channel at Felixstowe and proceeded east, arriving over Walcheren Island at 27,000ft (8,230m) hoping to entice the Fw 190s of II Gruppe, Jagdgeschwader 1 (II./JG1) at Woensdrecht up for combat. Capt. Leroy Gover led one element: "We took our P-47 Thunderbolts on their first operational trip today. We went into Holland at Flushing and flew along inland and came out at Dunkerque. The flak was pretty accurate. So all of the drinks are on the Republic representative here tonight." Although no enemy aircraft were sighted and none of the P-47Cs were hit by flak fired over Ostend and Blankenberge, the one hour and fifteen minute mission was the first of thousands launched across the globe: Thunderbolt had arrived.

First Blood

Fighter Sweep #204 was a late-afternoon fighter sweep from Furness, Netherlands, through Flushing and on to Cassel, France. It took off from Debden at 1635hrs on April 15, 1943, led by Maj. Donald Blakeslee, the 335th Fighter Squadron operations officer. "I left Felixstowe at 1701hrs on April 15, 1943, on course when I discovered that my gyro was unserviceable. Continuing by compass, I first saw the enemy coast near Knokke about 20 miles [32km] north of my intended landfall, flying at 29,060ft [8,857m].

I saw five vapor trails headed west about 5 miles [8km] north of Knokke and 5,000ft [1,524m] below us over the water. I made a turn to port and saw three Fw 190s below, flying southwest. As soon as they saw us, they turned inland and started home. Selecting the nearest one, who was in a 15-degree or 20-degree dive, I started down after him. Two unidentified P-47s took a short burst at him at long range and were overtaking him rapidly. His only evasive action was to increase his dive. I opened fire at about

Right and below: Lt. Col. Donald Blakeslee was the operations officer for the 4th Fighter Group. P-47C 41-6214 (below) was Blakeslee's mount when he scored the Thunderbolt's first aerial kill on April 15, 1943.

700yd [640m], closing to 500yd [457m], still firing. I saw tracers going over his canopy so I increased the angle of my dive and sawed him through twice. I saw many hits behind, on, and in front of the cockpit. He lurched sharply and a fraction of a second later, crashed into the ground, exploding. My entire attack was made from directly astern and slightly above. I pulled out of my dive below 500ft [152m] and found myself approaching Ostend. I went over the center of the city at about 300ft [91m] and was not fired on. Proceeding to about mid-Channel on the deck, I climbed to about 3,000ft [914m] and returned to base, landing at 1820. My number two was engaged when he was attempting to follow me down, but I returned home alone."

Blakeslee's flight dove into the attack with him, but as they passed through 20,000ft (6,096m) on the tail of the Focke-Wulf, another 190 bounced Lt. Happel from the left and Happel turned into him to engage. He fired about 100 rounds of .50-caliber at the Fw

Above: Lt. Jimmy Happel was flying as Blakeslee's wingman on Apri 15. Blakeslee was not impressed with the P-47, preferring the Spitfire's rate of climb and maneuverability over the Jug's speed and diving ability.

190, but did not see any results. Lt. Robert Boock, flying P-47C 41-6405 and leading the second element in Blakeslee's flight, followed as well: "I was flying toward our coast at 23,000ft [7,010m]. Lt. Happel was in front of me. I looked behind and a little above—a 190 was attacking a P-47. I did a wing over and the 190 did a split-S. I saw the P-47 struck and slide off into the haze. I allowed four rings of deflection [and fired] and the enemy aircraft burst into flames. I tried a burst at a second enemy aircraft, but he was out of range. I then followed the first down and saw him crash into the sea. Lt. Happel saw the crash around this time."

Although not on the mission, Capt. Leroy Gover kept a detailed diary while overseas and his entry for the April 15 mission was one of mixed emotions: "This afternoon there was a sweep to St. Omer. The squadron was bounced and both Anderson and McMinn were shot down. So goes another two of the boys. Lt. Col. Petersen was leading the wing and he had motor trouble and bailed out into the channel, but was picked up this evening. Maj. Blakeslee, Lt. Boock and Col. Petersen all got a 190."

GSAP — The Fighter Pilot's Insurance

Confirmation of a pilot's claims against enemy aircraft or ground targets was an essential part of closing out a mission. Installed in the leading edge of the P-47's right wing, the Gun Sight Aiming Point (GSAP) camera was boresighted to the airplane's .50-caliber machine guns and would be activated, provided the pilot turned it on, when he pulled the trigger. Three main types of GSAP were used from 1942 to 1945, and all used 16mm film in a removable cartridge. The original type M-4 ran on 12 volts, while the upgraded N-4 and AN/N-6 ran on 24 volts. The camera had three speeds, shooting at sixteen, thirty-two, or sixty-four frames per second and had three aperture settings that would be adjusted by the plane's armorer. The aperture settings were Bright, Hazy, or Dull, for clear, cloudy, or overcast/dusk conditions. The camera was powered on by a three-position covered switch in the cockpit. When the cover was engaged, the switch was in the center "off" position. The pilot could activate just the camera by moving the switch to the "up" position and then depressing the button on top of the control stick. Moving the switch to the "down" position would ensure that the camera would record whenever the guns were fired. Whenever a pilot had fired his guns on a combat mission, the GSAP film cartridge would be pulled and sent for developing at the squadron intelligence section. Once the developed film and pilot statements had been reviewed, and supporting information corroborated, confirmation or denial of a kill claim would be awarded.

Below: The N-6 16mm gun camera was mounted in the P-47's right wing root and was boresighted to film the exact point where fire from the airplane's eight .50-caliber machine guns converged.

Blitz Week

July 24, 1943, was the beginning of a week-long series of the largest 8th Air Force bombing raids yet, and P-47 groups were busy escorting the returning bombers. Thunderbolts on the July 30 mission to Kassel used external tanks for the first time, enabling them to venture even farther over the continent. In addition to extending the range of operations, the POINTBLANK directive, issued jointly by the RAF Bomber Command and the 8th Air Force on June 14, refocused the bombing campaign on the destruction of the German fighter force and its supporting industry. That July 30 morning, the 4th Bomb Wing launched 186 B-17s to hit Kassel and the 78th Fighter Group's squadrons rendezvoused with the bombers not a moment too soon.

Maj. Eugene Roberts, leading the 84th Fighter Squadron was first to spot the bomber stream: "I was flying as Group Leader on bomber withdrawal support on July 30, 1943. We took off with belly tanks and climbed to 23,000ft [7,010m] over the channel. Dropped tanks about 15 miles [24km] off the coast of Holland. Southeast of Noordwal we crossed the coast at 27,000ft [8,839m], indicating 180mph [289kmh]. Our course took us just north of Hellevotsluis over Dordrecht to the south of Nijmegen and just south of Haldern, the rendezvous point. We continued almost to Raesfeld. When we sighted the bombers off to our left, we made a 90-degree turn and picked up the bombers approximately over Winterswijk. One straggling bomber was observed, flying below the main formation in a dive, trailing black smoke and being attacked by about five enemy aircraft.

"I peeled my flight down and to the rear of the straggler. This would be about 1,000ft [305m] below the main formation of bombers and would be at about 21,000ft [6,400m]. All enemy aircraft sighted us and took evasive action to the extent that I was unable to close, although I did fire a burst with improper deflection. The enemy aircraft was in a diving attack from the rear on this straggler. I initiated my attack from the port side rear of the fighters, swinging in behind in their dive. They rolled to the left, then pulled up in a climbing turn to the right and broke sharply downward to the rear. I followed them in the climb, attempting to get a deflection shot. When he broke downward, I found I was directly beneath the bombers and saw a number of ball turret gunners firing at my flight. I broke down and to the rear, and pulled up to starboard side of the bombers about 1,000yd [914m] out, and at about their level. Looking up, I observed six enemy aircraft flying parallel to the bombers and about 1,000ft [305m] directly above me. They failed to see us and did not take any action, so after they passed, I made a climbing turn to the left to come up to their level and behind them. At this point I missed my second element and found myself alone with my wingman. In our pull up, we missed the original six enemy aircraft sighted, but sighted a single enemy aircraft ahead on the same level at about 1,500yd [1,372m]. I dived slightly below, opened full throttle, and closed to about 40yd [37m]. I pulled up directly behind the enemy aircraft and opened fire. Several strikes were observed on the

Below: The M2 tractor built by the Cleveland Tractor Company was the standard method of moving aircraft around the airfield when their engines weren't running.

behind, but the third burst caught him and he spun down, trailing smoke and flame some 1,500yd [1,372m] ahead of the bombers. I now found myself on the same level as the bombers and approaching them head on with no alternative other than to fly between their two main formations."

While Maj. Roberts was busy downing his third kill of the day, Capt. Charles P. London, who had scored his first three kills between June 24 and 29, brought down an additional Fw 190 and Me 109 to become the first of many P-47 aces. "The 83rd was on an escort mission with 180 B-17s and was scheduled to meet the bombers at Haldern on the way out from the target. We picked the bombers up even further into Germany as they were about ten minutes late. My section, Trumpcard Red and Blue Flights, were top cover at 31,000ft [9,449m]. There were about 100 enemy aircraft around the bombers. I saw two Fw 190s and four Me 109s fairly close to me at about 26,000ft [7,925m]. I attacked the 190s and fired at one of them, about a three-second burst, dead astern. I observed strikes on the fuselage and wings. Then he exploded and went down in flames.

"After I saw the 190 explode, I pulled up and after reaching about 28,000ft [8,534m], I saw an Me 109 below, going in behind the first box of bombers. I dove down and bounced, starting fire at 20 degrees deflection and closing to 0 degrees, at about 250yd [229m] astern. I saw strikes and flashes on the wings and fuselage. Then the 109 exploded."

Above: Lt. Gen. Jacob L. Devers presents the Distinguished Service Cross to Maj. Eugene P. Roberts, 84th Fighter Squadron, for his triple-kill mission of July 30, 1943.

Below: Thunderbolts of the 78th Fighter Group's 82nd Fighter Squadron are readied for their next mission from Duxford.

enemy aircraft, his wheels dropped and he spun down trailing a large volume of dark smoke and flame. I continued parallel to the bombers and sighted two more enemy aircraft about 2,000yd [1,828m] ahead. I used the same tactics, closing to 400yd [366m] astern, pulled up and opened fire on the port aircraft. I observed several strikes and the enemy aircraft billowed smoke and flame, rolled over, and went down. I was closing so fast that I had to pull up to avoid hitting him. I observed my wingman, F/O Koonts, firing at the second, or starboard aircraft, but did not see the results as he was under me. Both these aircraft were Fw 190s.

"After this second engagement, we were about 2 miles [3.4km] ahead of the bombers, still well out to their starboard side. About this time, I observed one enemy aircraft queuing up on port side and ahead of the bombers, so I cut across, falling in behind him. We started to close again using the same tactics as in the two previous attacks to get within range. This Me 109 peeled to starboard to attack the bombers head-on and I followed, closing to 500yd [457m] before opening fire. Two bursts were

The 56th's First Ace — Capt. Gerry Johnson

POINTBLANK moved the strategic air war into a new phase. Until this point, American and British bomber commands had sought to attack German industry in general; the Americans by day and the British at night. POINTBLANK sharpened the focus of the air campaign to go after the Luftwaffe fighter force, its airfields, and the industry that supported it.

On August 19, the 8th Air Force attacked the Luftwaffe fighter force directly. The 8th launched 125 B-17s to hit the airfields at Gilze-Rijn and Flushing in the Netherlands. Escorting the bombers were 175 P-47s from the 4th, 56th, and 78th Fighter Groups, which claimed nine enemy aircraft destroyed, two probably destroyed, and four damaged for the loss of one P-47. The 56th was to escort the bombers on their egress from the target area and were the most heavily engaged, claiming three Me 109s and one Fw 190 destroyed and one Me 109 damaged. Leading a flight of four Thunderbolts from the 61st Fighter Squadron, Capt. Gerald Johnson got his fifth kill, becoming the 8th Air Force's second ace and the first of many in the 56th Fighter Group.

"On August 19, 1943, I was leading Keyworth Blue Flight which was the first flight in the second section of our squadron. We crossed the coast going near Haamstede at 23,000ft [7,010m] and proceeded on course to meet the bombers. As we neared the first box of bombers I saw three unidentified planes flying parallel and on our left in the opposite direction at our altitude, 25,000ft [7,620m]. They made a large turn to the left and started in on our tail and at this point were about 2,000ft [610m] below us. I watched them come in and when they were about 1,000yd [914m] behind us I called a break to the left. We made a tight 360-degree turn and came out on their tail. They were Me 109s flying line abreast. As we made this turn, they continued flying straight with the exception that the leader did a very quick slow roll and then continued straight. I fired about a one-second burst from about 250yd [229m] at 15-degrees deflection at the number three plane. I saw strikes on the wing near the fuselage. He immediately flipped over and went straight down. I let him go and pulled up in a tight left turn and found the leader of these three straight in front of me at about 100yd [91m]. I started firing and he tried all kinds of maneuvers with the exception of breaking down as they ordinarily do. I could see flashes on his fuselage and I knew I was hitting him. Pretty soon there was a large red flash near the center of the fuselage and he started down in a rather steep dive, trailing smoke. I watched him go down for about 10,000ft [3,048m] and then pulled up to try to get my flight together again. Lt. Biales who was flying in the second flight in our section saw him hit the ground. Our flight was broken up so badly by these attacks that we couldn't rejoin so I joined Keyworth White Flight and completed the mission without further incident."

Above: *Capt. Gerald Johnson poses for a portrait in his full flying gear.By the end of the war and an exceptional combat career, Johnson was credited with 18.5 aerial victories, one probable, and 4.5 damaged*

1st Lt. Robert S. Johnson, who would eventually score twenty-two kills in the P-47 by war's end, was covering Capt. Gerald Johnson's wing on August 19 and scored his second kill on the mission. "I was flying Keyworth Blue Two. We were a little bit east and north of Woensdrecht when four Me 109s came in at us from the same level, about 25,000ft [7,620m] from about 5 o'clock. We had not quite reached the bombers. My leader turned left and pulled it slightly up. We made a 360-degree turn and came in at the Me 109s from about 7 o'clock to them. They had not turned from their original track, evidently thinking we were scared completely off. When they saw us coming, they rolled over and went in different directions but kept their altitude. One, the leader, pulled to the left and started climbing. Capt. Johnson, my leader, had begun to turn left after him. I followed slightly below my leader and not 25yd [23m] behind him. Capt. Johnson let a burst go and the Me 109 immediately broke right and spun. I was in good position then and fired at him in the slow spin. I saw strikes and smoke began to come from him. He pulled out of the spin and started straight down. Capt. Johnson had pulled up and I thought he was watching it and my tail, so I rolled over and going straight down on his tail, I opened up again. Strikes were seen all over him and very much more smoke poured out. I tried to pull out as he went slightly to the left in a steep dive. I was gaining speed rapidly and my ship shuddered all over. As I finally pulled it out at from 12,000 to 15,000ft [3,658 to 4,752m] I saw the pilot also being in a very shallow dive, rolled on his side and a chute opened. The Me 109 then plowed into the ground and I returned to the P-47s above the bombers."

Left: The first of many—Capt. Gerald Johnson scored his fifth kill on August 19, 1943, and became the 56th Fighter Group's first ace. As the tally here shows, five kills was just the beginning.

It was clear that the P-47 was starting to have a positive effect on operations. After the October 8, 1943, mission to Bremen, Headquarters US Army Air Force released a memo that was then distributed throughout the state-side training commands like I Fighter Command. It stated that: "There are those who believe this war will be won or lost by the aircraft now in use. They remark that it takes a long time to design and produce the best new military planes and assert that those now in service will have to be modified and improved to meet the new conditions. If they are right, then out use of the Thunderbolts may prove to be the tactics to which the Germans are unable to find a counter, for these fighters are a match for any Nazi fighters they can reach."

Below: Lt. Bob Johnson was flying Capt. Eugene O'Neill's P-47 aircraft "Torchy" on the August 19, 1943, mission when he scored the second of his ultimately impressive twenty-two wartime kills.

That's a heck of a role for a fighter!
The 5th Emergency Rescue Squadron

"According to Tom, they lost me initially in all those whitecaps. It took twenty minutes till they finally found me again. Then the P-47s from Air-Sea Rescue marked my spot with smoke bombs and dye. Tom said when they finally located me, I looked like a drowning rat hanging onto a doughnut. I tried to wave once and let him know I was alive, but in the attempt, I nearly drowned."

—Lt. Stephen C. Ananian, 505th Fighter Squadron, October 5, 1944

Above: This British-made whistle would have been worn on the hook closure at the neck of an A-2 flight jacket.

"War weary" airplanes—those airframes that had surpassed their planned service life and had been replaced by updated models—were still useful. Suddenly the P-47s that had been critically short on range over Europe were able to loiter over the English Channel at low to medium altitude for hours, while their pilots coordinated the rescue of downed aircrews in the Channel. Originally the 8th Air Force was content to use British Air-Sea Rescue (ASR) services, but it quickly became apparent that an American equivalent was needed. It took all of June 1943 to establish the 8th Air Force ASR service and the first mission was conducted entirely by US personnel on July 4.

The Spotter Service idea had been pioneered by the British and was conducted by a flight of two fighters as soon as a ditching was reported. The fighter element would be vectored toward the last known position of the ditched aircraft. The fighters' speed was the key factor, as they could reach the scene quickly and locate survivors. Loitering over the downed crew, the fighter would report their location to the slower rescue aircraft or surface vessels. Originally these fighters were pulled from operational units, but due to a few instances of spotter fighters not being available, it was clear dedicated aircraft were needed.

Detachment B, 65th Fighter Wing—redesignated the 5th Emergency Rescue Squadron (ERS) in January 1945—was established on May 8, 1944, under the command of Capt. Robert Gerhart and was to be equipped with forty-two war-weary P-47s. Direct radio links to both USAAF and RAF rescue services were established, and within a week, the detachment had received twenty-five veteran Thunderbolts and begun flying spotter missions.

Below: ERS Thunderbolts operated in teams of two, with one airplane remaining at altitude, serving as a radio relay aircraft, while the other conducted a low-altitude search for downed aircrew.

The squadron's Thunderbolts were specially adapted for their unusual mission. Four .50-caliber machine guns were removed, lightening the P-47's takeoff weight by over 600lb (272kg), improving fuel consumption. They carried special air-droppable life-raft packs on underwing bomb racks and a 108-gal (408-liter) external fuel tank on the centerline station. Aft of the external tank was a special smoke bomb rack for marking downed aircraft positions. After some experimentation, this loadout gave the Thunderbolt crews the most flexibility and a five-hour flight duration.

Their mission had four major components:
- Intercept aircraft in distress while still in the air and lead them to safety
- Locate downed aircraft
- Maintain contact with the downed aircrew and relay information
- Escort and protect the rescue aircraft.

Arriving over an aircraft's last known location, a typical flight would split up, one fighter staying at altitude to provide cover and act as a radio relay aircraft for the low plane. From there, the low airplane, flying only at a few hundred feet, would begin a box search pattern. Low and slow

Above: War weary P-47D-15-RE 42-75855 (in this and the previous photo), along with the squadron's other Thunderbolts, were painted to be as visible as possible.

was the only method for spotting a downed pilot or aircrew, and as a result search patterns were flown at about 170mph (277kmh) to allow pilots the necessary time to spot a tiny dinghy in the choppy waters of the English Channel.

In January 1945, the 5th ERS became an official squadron with a Table of Organization & Equipment (TO&E). The squadron received its own OA-10A Catalina rescue aircraft, greatly simplifying their ability to locate and rescue downed aircrews. Now a flight of four Thunderbolts could launch with a single OA-10. Two P-47s would speed ahead and intercept the aircraft in distress or locate the ditching site, while the second pair escorted the OA-10 to the rendezvous point. In a number of cases, the rescue aircraft, escorted by P-47s, arrived just as the downed aircrew were exiting their aircraft, having just ditched in the Channel. The 5th ERS was unique in the USAAF, as it was the only ERS to employ fighter aircraft in the spotter role.

Second Schweinfurt – 353rd Fighter Group

The second raid on the ball-bearing factories at Schweinfurt on October 14, 1943, has become known as the mission that nearly broke the 8th Air Force. While the P-47s with external tanks were ranging farther from England than ever before, they still lacked the endurance to escort the bombers deep into Germany, fight the Luftwaffe, and then return to England while defending the bombers.

The 353rd Fighter Group was covering the first waves of bombers en route to the target. While the P-47s were able to protect the bombers to an extent, coverage was thin, and B-17 losses were cripplingly heavy. The Luftwaffe sustained fairly heavy fighter losses though, and Maj. Walter Beckham claimed his fifth and sixth kills.

"I was leading Roughman Blue Flight flying at 28,000 to 29,000ft [8,534 to 8,839m] above and on the right hand edge of the bombers. We were in the vicinity of Aachen (guessing from elapsed time only, as we were over an overcast). Twenty-plus 190s came in toward the

Left: Lt. Col. Ben Rimerman and Maj. Walter Beckham conversing in front of Beckham's P-47D-5-RE "Little Demon" after a successful mission.

bombers at their same level and from three o'clock. I announced them on the R/T and heard someone else also calling them in. They were flying very nearly in line abreast.

"We went out toward them at our altitude (about 28,000ft [8,534m]) and made a steep diving turn to the right and came out almost on top of them. I shot one that had a belly tank from astern, closing to just behind him, seeing strikes, pieces, and smoke. Believe that his belly tank was one of those pieces. Lt. W. J. Maguire, my number 2 observed the action.

"[I] Made a slight right turn and shot another one from the rear and close range. Many pieces came off and he rolled over slowly to the right and started down on fire. Lt. Maguire called me that he had one on his tail at this point. I turned as sharply as I could to the left and saw a 190 behind him. I would have been able to make a head on attack, but he pushed his nose downward, avoiding action.

"Lt. Maguire called me, stating he was going after this enemy aircraft. Unfortunately I did not receive his transmission so failed to stay with him,

Below: External fuel tanks allowed the Thunderbolt to range all the way to Germany. The Emden raid of September 27, 1943, was the first raid where P-47s accompanied the bombers all the way to Germany.

THE STARS AND STRIPES

1D · 1D

Daily Newspaper of U.S. Armed Forces

in the European Theater of Operations

New York, N.Y.—London, England

Tuesday, Sept. 28, 1943

Vol. 3 No. 281

Reds Cross Dnieper In Drive West

viets Seize 1,100 Places; Armies 85 Miles from Poland in North

viet paratroopers carried the c Russian offensive to the west s of the Dnieper yesterday as main armies were liberating places from the Germans in the westward.

Polish border was only 85 rom several points along the

Marine Shows New Rank With British Insignia

Max Dunlap, U.S. Marine combat correspondent in England, recently promoted from staff sergeant to Marine gunner, has had to resort to British insignia to show his new rank, the equivalent of the Army's warrant officer.

As far as anyone knows, Dunlap is the only man with that rank in the ETO, and because the marine quartermaster stocks in England are small, he has taken the stripes off his GI blouse and bought British Royal Engineer lapel insignia which look something like Marine shoulder insignia for the gunner rank after the Latin motto of the Royal Engineers has been broken off the bottom.

Meanwhile, guards at ETO headquarters are puzzled whether to

Flying Forts Hammer Emden, Vital German Merchant Port; P47 Escorts Go All the Way

P47s Shoot Down 22 Fighters In Longest Escort Assignment

Three Thunderbolt Pilots Get Two Jerries Each On 600-Mile Flight, First to Escort Forts All the Way to Target

Eighth Air Force P47 Thunderbolts shot down 22 German interceptors

Huge USAAF Force Dropped at Least 1,000 Tons

Flying Fortresses literally plastered the German naval base of Emden yesterday while Marauders of the USAAF smashed for the fifth time in ten days at the Beauvais-Tille air-

Above: Maj. Beckham's gun camera footage showing an Me 109's dramatic last moments, fragmenting under the P-47 gunfire.

thinking that he was still following me. Shortly after, I thought I heard a call from Lt. Maguire, turned half around and saw flaming pieces of an aircraft falling that may have been this same one which was destroyed by Lt. Maguire.

"I am not sure whether the rest of the original twenty-plus enemy aircraft were able to complete the attack on the Forts, but I am sure that six or eight of them did not. The action took place between 23,000 and 24,000ft [7,010 and 7,315m] and I fired 846 rounds with one stoppage. I wish to commend Lt. Maguire for staying right in there advising me that our tail was clear, then calmly announcing that one was on his tail and then shooting him down after that attack was diverted."

Lt. Maguire was initially in trouble, but managed to turn the tables on his attacker: "Checking my tail again, I saw an Fw 190 closing in on me from 7 o'clock. I called Capt. Beckham on the radio and asked for help. Capt. Beckham broke around to the left and I pulled up and over him,

going around the enemy aircraft. Capt. Beckham missed this enemy aircraft and started climbing up to the right of the Focke-Wulf. I called him and said I would get the enemy aircraft. Closing fast, I fired a burst from about 350yd [320m], dead astern. I saw strikes and pieces fly off. It had a belly tank which went off, also a large piece of the underside. I moved in to about 200yd [183m] and fired another long burst noticing strikes on the wings and tail assembly of the enemy aircraft, which started to break up. Thinking I would run through the parts of the enemy aircraft, I pulled up to avoid hitting them. As I looked back, I saw the main part of the Fw 190 going down in flames and big pieces still falling off of it. It took no evasive action, I believe one of my bursts must have killed the pilot. I pulled up and to the right looking for Capt. Beckham, but I did not see him so I headed home."

Capt. Orville Kinkade was leading Roughman Red Flight and was above and behind Beckham's Blue Flight when the bandits were first spotted. "We S'ed over the bombers to the front of the box, turned and flew back to the last box, where the bandits were reported. I saw four 109s off to our right at about 32,000ft [9,753m]. Making a tight circle to gain altitude, I saw another flight of P-47s bounce the enemy aircraft, forcing them down in pairs. Two of the enemy aircraft broke to our left at which time I took several short bursts at the leader at about 500yd [457m].

I made a left turn and followed them down, closing rapidly on the leading enemy aircraft. I opened fire at about ten degrees deflection, 300yd [274m]. I noticed strikes on the tail assembly and fuselage behind the cockpit, noticing large pieces falling off. As I closed in to about 200yd [182m], I fired another long burst, seeing strikes on the engine, right wing, and fuselage and again, pieces fell off. My next burst from about the same range evidently killed the pilot because I noticed strikes hitting the cockpit. The canopy flew off and that part of the plane disintegrated. As I pulled up, I saw a large sheet of flame on the right side of the aircraft and no parachute was seen."

Of the 291 B-17s launched on the raid, sixty were shot down either by flak or fighters. Another seven returned to England, but were too badly damaged to repair, and an additional 138 airplanes were damaged on the raid. With nearly one third of the attacking force destroyed and more than 500 airmen taken prisoner, the 8th Air Force temporarily suspended operations to re-evaluate the effectiveness of strategic daylight bombing.

Expanded Operations

"I was watching an enemy aircraft 3,000ft [914m] below at
11 o'clock when another enemy aircraft attacked from 2 o'clock
above, overshooting and allowing me to turn in on his tail.
I opened fire at 700yd [640m], closing to 150yd [137m],
observing many hits on the fuselage and wing roots."

—Capt. Robert Sedman, 374th Fighter Squadron, January 30, 1944

Late 1943 saw several major reorganizations of the USAAF formations arrayed against Germany. A new numbered air force, the 15th, was created in the Mediterranean Theater in November 1943 to increase strategic pressure on German industry and on the Luftwaffe. In England, VIII Fighter Command more than doubled the number of P-47 groups by the end of the year, adding the 352nd, 355th, 356th, 358th, 359th, and 361st Fighter Groups to further expand 8th Air Force offensive operations.

The new P-51B Mustang also began arriving in-theater by late fall 1943 and started flying combat missions with the 4th and 354th (borrowed from the 9th Air Force) Fighter Groups in December. With the Mustang's greater range, VIII Fighter Command finally had the escort fighter needed for return trips to Germany. But another significant development in the fall of 1943 was the introduction of the P-47D-15-RE. The new version was the first production variant to feature factory-installed underwing pylons for external wing tanks. These further extended the P-47's range another 150 miles (241km) when two 108-gal (409-liter) drop tanks were carried.

With the Mustang's selection as the 8th Air Force's escort fighter, the P-47 groups all began to transition to the new fighter in early 1944. Several of those groups recently arrived in England would only fly the Thunderbolt in combat for a few months before trading them in for new Mustangs. The 361st, for example, flew its first combat mission on January 21, 1944, and less than five months later flew its first all-Mustang mission on May 13. The 352nd and 355th both traded in their trusty Thunderbolts after only nine months of operations.

However, the Thunderbolt's war was by no means winding down. As 8th Air Force groups transitioned to the Mustang, the 9th Air Force and its three Tactical Air Commands (IX, XIX, and XXIX TAC) were accepting former 8th Air Force airplanes at an incredible pace. These worn and battle-weary airplanes became the core of the 9th Air Force for the first few months of 1944, until units like the 358th and 362nd Fighter Groups began receiving new production airframes from the United States. New aircraft never fully replaced those original war horses, and it was not uncommon to find early block Thunderbolts flying combat missions through the spring of 1945.

The transition from strategic escort to tactical fighter-bomber in the European Theater of Operations (ETO) was never fully completed, as the 56th Fighter Group remained on escort duty, flying Thunderbolts throughout the remainder of the war. However, they were the exception to the rule that P-47s were low- to medium-altitude tactical aircraft, while the P-51 was the long-range escort.

Left: Staggered escort was the best option over Europe: one group to escort the bombers to target, another to cover them through the target and egress, and a third group to provide withdrawal support.

Achtung Zerstörer!

The 352nd Fighter Group had arrived in England in August 1943 and flew its first combat mission on September 9, providing withdrawal support to B-17s returning from various targets in France. A similar mission on December 22 netted the group's 328th Fighter Squadron three confirmed kills.

While covering three straggling B-17s returning from the Osnabruck marshaling yards, Maj. Everett Stewart's Turndown White Flight spotted a pair of Me 109s approaching the bombers from the rear, running in fast. "As I came back down through the cloud, evidently the enemy aircraft spotted our flight starting the bounce and broke for the deck, disappearing into the low overcast at about 10,000ft [3,048m]. We remained in the vicinity for a few minutes and when they didn't reappear, we continued covering the Forts."

Fifteen minutes later, at 1500hrs, Maj. Stewart's flight was up at 23,000ft [7,010m] and spotted a pair of Messerschmitt 110s "below us at about 3 o'clock down sun. We bounced them, and as I closed in fast on the Me 110 to the rear and right of the pair, I took two or three three-second bursts at about 5 degrees deflection. I closed from 350 to 150yd [320 to 137m] and noticed strikes around the cockpit area. As I was

overrunning, I called Lt. Coleman (White 3) to take him, whereupon I slid over to the lead Me 110 and fired three three-to-four-second bursts with slight deflection, observing strikes all over the aircraft. Meanwhile, Lt. Powell (White 2) had moved in on my left wing slightly below me and almost dead astern of the enemy aircraft. On my last burst on this Me 110, Lt. Powell and I were both hitting the airplane in motor sections and cockpit. Parts were flying from the aircraft and the port engine was burning as I pulled over to let Lt. Powell finish him off if it needed it. I then turned back over Lt. Coleman who was still firing at the first Me 110 we had fired on. The aircraft was smoking and as I pulled into formation with Lt. Coleman, we flew through much debris from it. I pulled up and watched the enemy aircraft (by this time burning) roll over on its back, canopy and other parts falling off. It then dropped off into a vertical dive into the clouds, burning fiercely."

Lt. Robert "Punchy" Powell, covering Maj. Stewart's wing, followed his lead in the initial bounce on the pair of Me 110s. "Maj. Stewart and I opened fire almost together on the second enemy aircraft, catching it in a cross fire from about 300yd [274m] and closing in to 150yd [137m]. I

Above: *Pilots and crew of the 352nd Fighter Group's 487th Fighter Squadron appear in relaxed mood for this posed photograph. The fuselage art indicates the number of escort missions flown.*

Above: *Renowned 352nd Fighter Group Mustang ace Maj. George Preddy (see here on the left) actually scored his first three kills in the Thunderbolt, demonstrating the aircraft's competence as a pure fighter aircraft.*

constant hits, many parts of the aircraft falling off—engine hoods, canopy, etc. By this time both engines were smoking badly and I saw flames. He then flipped over on his back and went vertically into the overcast."

With two Me 110s destroyed, Maj. Stewart called for the flight to regroup on him. But five minutes later, more bandits were sighted: "I spotted two enemy aircraft about 500ft [152m] below us on our left and as I did, Lt. Coleman and Lt. Horne broke right into a third Me 110 I hadn't seen. As I approached the two Lt. Powell and I bounced, I observed one Me 110 in the lead and an Me 210 behind and to the right of him. They saw us bouncing and started down to the clouds." Stewart saw strikes on the airplane, but was unable to justify more than a "damaged" claim.

Lt. Horne, however, had better luck. "The second encounter was also a combat action led by Maj. Stewart. Two enemy aircraft were coming in at about one o'clock and a little below. We had climbed back to 14,000ft [4,267m] after the first bounce. Maj. Stewart and Lt. Powell broke left to bounce the one on the right and Lt. Coleman and I broke right to attack the one on the left, at which time the enemy aircraft (an Me 210 and an Me 110) were flying east. I followed Lt. Coleman a little high, and at that moment a third ship appeared from out of a cloud slightly under me. My cockpit was filled with smoke and it was difficult to tell whether the Me 110 was smoking or pulling streams, so I opened fire at 250yd [229m], closing to 150yd [137m] before breaking. I last saw the ship explode in the top of the clouds."

The 352nd continued to build an impressive combat record over the subsequent months, scoring multiple kills on a number of occasions. By mid-April 1944, the group began transitioning to the P-51 and adopted what became their identifying feature, the famous "Blue-nosed Bastards of Bodney."

Above: *Maj. Everett Stewart's gun camera footage clearly shows Lt. Powell's P-47 delivering the coup de grace on the doomed Me 110.*
Right: *"Lucky Strike"—the serviceman's favourite.*

observed many strikes on the Me 110's wing roots, fuselage, canopy, and engines. Maj. Stewart called me and told me to follow the 110 down and, still firing and observing hits, I saw him disappear in a puff of his own smoke. I rejoined Maj. Stewart just in time to observe Lt. Coleman destroy the first Me 110. It seemed to be falling apart and flipped over, dropping out of sight."

Things looked similar from the flight's second element. "We peeled off for the bounce, but found we were going too fast for a good burn. Maj. Stewart called, 'I'm going to overshoot; you take them, Johnny,' but managed to skid into position, losing speed at the same time. I pulled up in line abreast and watched strikes on the left engine of the second enemy aircraft which broke to the left. I then moved behind the leading Me 110 at about 300yd [274m] and opened fire, seeing strikes on the fuselage and left wing and engine. He went into a violent skid and then dived for the cloud level below. I continued to fire and had

The Brunswick raid – January 30, 1944

The 361st Fighter Group was one of the last P-47 groups assigned to the 8th Air Force, arriving in England in December 1943 and commencing operations in early January. January 30 saw the first air-to-air engagement for the 361st's 374th Fighter Squadron, which made the group's first claims against the Luftwaffe while waiting to cover the withdrawal of the largest 8th Air Force bombing raid yet: the 778-plane strike on Braunschweig (or Brunswick), Germany.

Maj. Roy Webb led the 374th and was the first to engage: "I was leading Hubbard Squadron at 28,000ft [8,534m] in the Rheine area when approximately twenty Me 109Gs approached from 30,000ft [9,144m] attacking us out of the sun. I made a tight turn to the right and then broke left into a left Lufberry [a maneuver where a defending formation flies in a horizontal circle in order that lead and trail aircraft can better acquire and engage attacking aircraft]. The enemy aircraft attacked the rear flight from 4 o'clock and the squadron then broke up into flights. Observing an enemy aircraft on Lt. Calloway's tail (Blue Flight #2) I made a left wing-over down on the enemy aircraft's tail. The 109 broke right down followed by a left wing-over, I followed closing rapidly at 18,000ft [5,486m] and opened fire at 300yd [274m], closing to 100ft [30m]. I saw strikes on the wing roots, canopy, tail section, and the wings. I then broke up left and saw the enemy aircraft going straight down, apparently out of control. The 109's canopy was seen to fly off and the plane started flaming."

Capt. Robert Sedman claimed the next enemy planes shot down that day. "I was leading Hubbard Red Flight in the Rheine area at 25,000ft [7,620m] orbiting right in search of bombers. Contrails were reported above. We watched the contrails pass over us and went into a Lufberry. At this time, twenty-five Me 109Gs attacked out of the sun from 30,000ft [9,144m], coming down from all directions. One enemy aircraft approached my flight from 1 o'clock, out of

Left: Maj. Roy Webb, CO of the 374th Fighter Squadron, taking a nap after an early 1944 mission.

range, but I turned into him and gave him a short burst to check my guns. At this time, an enemy aircraft was reported by my wingman Lt. Lederer, to be attacking Yellow Flight from dead astern at 200yd [183m]. I broke on the enemy aircraft's tail causing him to break off straight down. I did a violent push-over and followed the enemy aircraft down. At 15,000ft [4,571m], I opened fire at extreme range and closed to approximately 350yd [320m], observing hits at the wing roots and fuselage. I leveled off at 2,000ft [610m] and observed the enemy aircraft passing under my wing, going straight down presumably out of control.

"I zoomed back up to 11,000ft [3,353m] noticing several friendly aircraft in the vicinity. I attempted by radio to reform my flight and four aircraft formed up on my wing at 12,000ft [3,658m]. I was watching an enemy aircraft 3,000ft [914m] below at 11 o'clock when another enemy aircraft attacked from 2 o'clock above, overshooting and allowing me to turn in on his tail. I opened fire at 700yd [640m], closing to 150yd [137m], observing many hits on the fuselage and wing roots. As I broke right and up, I flew through pieces from the aircraft one of which punched a hole in my engine cowling. The enemy aircraft fell off into a diving left turn and the pilot was observed to bail out."

Right: P-47D-22-RE 42-25969 was assigned to Lt. John D. Duncan of the 376th Fighter Squadron. Duncan scored his only air-to-air kill in a P-47 on February 25, 1944.

Right: Pilots might wear A-6A fleece-lined flight boots, but at low or medium altitudes often wore standard "roughout" low boots.

Locke. I followed Lt. Amason into the dive and during the dive recovery I lost sight of him. I did not see him again."

Hastin took over the number three position, but quickly attacked another Messerschmitt, not seeing the Thunderbolt just below him. "I was about 7,000ft [2,134m] indicating 500mph [805kmh] and I observed an Me 109G at 2 o'clock, 1,500ft [457m] below me. I fell off right in a shallow dive, dead astern of the enemy aircraft, opening fire at 600yd [549m] and breaking off at 100yd [91m]. I observed strikes on the left wing root and cockpit. The enemy aircraft broke down and left and I noticed a small explosion in the vicinity of the cockpit. As I broke up and right, I noticed Lt. Lederer, Red 2, directly beneath me, not more than 10ft [3m]. Lt. Lederer had been shooting at the same aircraft, but I was unable to observe his fire. The last I saw of the enemy aircraft, he was headed straight down apparently out of control at 2,500ft [762m]."

The 374th was credited with four Me 109s destroyed on the 30th, but also saw their first loss at the hands of the enemy, as Lt. Amason never rejoined the flight. Amason was the first of ten pilots lost during the 361st's four-month tenure with the P-47.

Lt. Lederer, flying Capt. Sedman's wing, was able to get in position on another Messerschmitt. "Immediately following these attacks, another Me 109G was observed off my left wing. I called Capt. Sedman on the radio and asked him to cover my tail and I went in on the enemy aircraft's tail at about 6,000ft [1,829m] indicating 550mph [885kmh]. At the same time, Lt. Hastin was approaching the same enemy aircraft from the right and above. Lt. Hastin, Red Four, was a few feet above me on my right and slightly behind. I opened fire on the enemy aircraft at about 150yd [137m], observing strikes on the left wing foot and left side of the fuselage. Lt. Hastin was firing at the same time. Pieces of the enemy aircraft fell off and hit my right wing, ring cowling, propeller, and smashed the right side of my windshield. The enemy aircraft was observed to go into a diving turn to the left and I last saw him in a vertical dive going into the overcast."

During the initial attack, Lt. James Hastin had become separated from his element leader, 1st Lt. Ethelbert Amason, but was able to remain with the rest of the flight. "Capt. Sedman led the flight in a dive down from 24,000ft [7,315m] to attack an Me 109 that was attacking Lt.

Below: An impressive lineup of 361st Fighter Group Thunderbolts, ready for action in early spring 1944.

"Trooptrain" Thunderbolts

While the POINTBLANK directive concentrated the 8th Air Force bombing raids on the German fighter force and the industry that supported it, as the planned invasion of the European continent drew nearer, the 8th shifted focus to begin restricting German movement to western France. "Big Week" began on February 20, 1944, and was a series of daily, round-the-clock bombing raids undertaken by both the 8th Air Force and RAF Bomber Command.

The raids continued once the week was out, however, and the March 2, 1944, raid on the Frankfurt marshaling yards was intended to destroy as much rolling stock as possible. Knocking out, or at least severely damaging, one of the key German rail hubs that could rush reinforcements to the invasion front was critical for the invasion's success. The March 2 raid launched 481 B-17s and B-24s, but due to poor weather and navigational errors, only one third of the bombers struck the intended target. The remaining two-thirds attacked secondary targets around Frankfurt.

Thunderbolts of the 358th Fighter Squadron, callsign "Trooptrain," were assigned to escort the 2nd Bomb Wing's B-24s and were to link up with the last box of bombers as they withdrew after dropping their bombs. Maj. Raymond Myers, the squadron commander, was "leading Red Flight of Trooptrain Squadron heading east at 23,000ft [7,010m] looking for the last combat wing of B-24s. We spotted three Me 109s at 1420hrs heading north about 500ft [152m] below us and two other enemy aircraft at about 4 o'clock low to us. I dispatched Green Flight to bounce them with Blue Flight to cover, while my Red Flight went on to bounce the three Me 109s we spotted with Yellow Flight to cover us.

Below: "Armed Services Edition" paperback novels, free from the USO.

"We turned into them in trail from out of the sun and I called my flight to close up so that we could get all three and in about three–four minutes, we closed. They took no evasive action from the very start of the bounce until we closed. I singled out the straggler who was on the left hand side and started firing from dead astern from about 300yd [274m], riding in his prop wash all the time. He then cut his throttle and I cut mine, but had to stop firing at 50ft [15m] or less. I came so close to him, I almost chewed his tail off and then pulled up to the left, slid over to the right, and came back down on him with about a 20-degree deflection shot. He was last seen in a steep dive, apparently out of control and smoking. I was at about 10,000ft [3,047m]."

Myers' wingman, Lt. Charles Blair, also claimed a Messerschmitt: "Our flight began a bounce from out of the sun and chased the 109s for about three–four minutes, closing to about 250yd [229m]. Maj. Myers opened fire on the left wingman, so I moved over to line myself up on the right wingman, 200yd [183m] behind him and closing and then began firing. I saw strikes on the left side of the fuselage and the cockpit. The enemy

Left: This P-47D-2 from the 358th Fighter Squadron was likely one of the few Thunderbolts retained by the 355th Fighter Group as "Bill's Buzz Boys," a dedicated strafing element in spring 1944.

Above: B-17F 42-30226 "Spook V" of the 95th Bomb Group's 336th Bomb Squadron. The P-47 escort a thousand feet above the bombers provided top cover against marauding German fighters.

Right: Pitot tube, machine guns, and clouds—a P-47 escort pilot's view out of the left side of his canopy.

aircraft shot upward and fell off on the right wing. I followed him down to 6,000ft [1,829m] or lower. He was still going straight down when I pulled off."

The third Messerschmitt was equally unaware of the Trooptrain Thunderbolts and Lt. Harold Hoffman, leading the second Red Flight element, crossed over and passed Maj. Myers and "got on the leader, letting our Red #2 man take the one on the extreme right. I gave the enemy aircraft a burst and observed strikes on his fuselage and left wing, which caused smoke to pour from it. He made a mild turn left, and I gave him a long burst. I closed approximately 75yd [69m], getting many strikes and causing a mild explosion followed by a puff of flame and lots of smoke. I broke off my attack, since he was headed for the ground and burning."

While Red Flight engaged and destroyed the three Messerschmitts, Trooptrain Green Flight went after the pair of Fw 190s. Unbeknown to the flight leader, 1st Lt. Walter Gresham, the Focke-Wulf leader was 103-

kill *Experte*, Oberstleutnant Egon Mayer, Geschwaderkommodore (wing commander) of JG2. Mayer was the first German ace to reach one hundred kills solely on the Western Front and had twelve P-47s to his credit. Gresham's flight, however had caught Mayer unaware: "We started a bounce from out of the sun at 1420hrs. The two enemy aircraft split, one going to the right and the other to the left. I told Green 3 and 4 to take the second enemy aircraft while I took the leader who was in a left turn. I gave him a short burst at 400–500yd [366–457m] and closed to 300yd [274m] and opened fire. Hits were seen in and around his cockpit and on both wings. I saw an explosion on the right wing root and about this time almost half of his left wing disintegrated and broke off completely. The enemy aircraft, identified as an Fw 190, snapped and did a half cartwheel and then went into a violent spin. The combat took place between 15,000 and 12,000ft [4,571 and 3,658m] and at the time of the attack I was indicating 500mph [805kmh] and not closing too fast."

Lt. Roscoe Fussell and Flight Officer Lawrence Dudley quickly chased down Mayer's wingman. Fussell fired until he was about 100yd [91m] out, but had to break contact, allowing a clear shot for F/O Dudley. Both pilots observed hits on the forward fuselage and wing roots, ultimately forcing the pilot to bail out and sending the second Fw 190 down in flames.

Chow Time

"With the coming of very hot weather, ice-cream freezers have suddenly gone into mass production. A number of the departments have invented their own and have had castings made in Hsien for parts they were unable to obtain."

—Group Monthly Report, 81st Fighter Group, Hsien, China

In early 1943, the pilots of the 4th Fighter Group were forced to give up their beloved Spitfires for the huge and yet-unproven Thunderbolt. However, with the shift in airframe came a shift in group logistics. Until that point, the group was dependent on the British for spare parts, rations, and equipment. Yet on February 1, according to the group intelligence officer, "The officer's mess changed from British to American rations. Farewell to sprouts, cabbage, kippers, and imitation sausage. The officers go on American rations with a sigh of relief, but a dubious look in their eyes over the increased cost."

The 8th Air Force pilots and ground crews ate

better than most of their counterparts in the other numbered air forces. After a grueling five-hour mission over Europe, pilots were able to stop at the mess hall, get some hot chow, and unwind from the day's mission. As the Allied armies pushed across Europe and up the Italian boot, however, the 9th and 12th Air Forces moved along to shorten the distance between base and frontlines. In doing so, air and ground crews often found themselves eating boxed K-rations while headed to a new airfield. C and K rations would be the standard fare until the squadron and group field kitchens arrived and set up for operations.

The living conditions in China were surprisingly first-rate, and the members of the 81st Fighter Group ate very well while stationed in Hsien, China. "Barracks Number 5 of this squadron recently gave a buffet supper and ice-cream party with each participant consuming on the average a menu of sardines, tuna fish, ripe olives, potted meat, cheese, kippered herring, mayonnaise, saltines, cheese tidbits, bread, anchovies, fruit juices, and about two quarts of chocolate ice cream."

In the Central Pacific, like in China, ice cream was a precious commodity and Mess Sections guarded their prized equipment. On Ie Shima in June 1945, the 464th Fighter Squadron mess was set up on the west side of the squadron area. "A kitchen was erected by putting plywood wing tank boxes over a framework of 2 x 4 lumber. A squadron

Both above: The ETO 8th Air Force crews were fortunate to have buildings to serve as their pilot and crew mess, while on Saipan (pictured here), crews had an open-sided mess tent. Here we also see the M1937 field stove.

tent was used as the roof. Field ranges and other equipment were set up and rations were drawn on a day-by-day basis. Several times during the month fresh meat and butter was received off a refrigerator ship. After several futile tries and break-downs, ice cream was made in the squadron ice cream machine, which was set up in a special building at the east side of the kitchen. The biggest difficulty at the end of the month was securing the necessary ingredients like sugar and milk."

In addition to setting up a kitchen, a tarp was hung between trees as a shelter for a dining room. The tables were made from wing tank crates and .50-caliber ammunition boxes were used as seats. The first part of the month, officers ate with the enlisted men. An officers' mess was opened up north of the officers' area for all group officers later in the month. Cooks and mess personnel were supplied by the squadrons.

K and C rations

K rations came in a cardboard box measuring roughly 7 x 4 x 2in (18 x 10 x 6cm), with a sealed wax paper pouch inside. Inside the waterproof pouch would be a small tin of meat, some crackers, bouillon cubes, Charms candy, powdered coffee, a small pack of four cigarettes, a can opener, spoon, and toilet paper. While not as desirable as hot chow, the K ration provided sustenance in the field far better than standard rations of both other Allied and Axis armies. Canned C rations were also available and were somewhat favored over the K rations. These were individual cans, each containing a different meal, like meat and vegetable stew, spaghetti and meat sauce, chicken and vegetables, or franks and beans. The 333rd Fighter Squadron was issued both C and K rations while waiting for the construction of a mess hall on Ie Shima and the C rations were popular.

Right and below: K rations came in Breakfast, Dinner, and Supper meals and included cigarettes, toilet paper, charms candies, bouillon cubes, and instant coffee, in addition to the meal's entrée. Below we see preparation for Thanksgiving.

Breakfast

Meat and Eggs: eat cold, or after heating by boiling can in water. Biscuits • Coffee
Cereal: eat dry or crumble into canteen cup and add hot or cold water.
Fruit Bar: eat cold or make into jam by stewing 3 to 5 minutes in about 4 spoonfuls of water.
Sugar • Chewing Gum • Cigarettes

Blue Leader

As the Allied buildup of 1944 continued and the Mustang became the standard mount of the 8th Air Force, the 9th Air Force quickly became the largest operator of the Thunderbolt over the Normandy beachhead and beyond.

Capt. Cowell Van Deventer had joined the Royal Canadian Air Force (RCAF) in 1941 and then transferred over to the USAAF when the United States entered the war. During his three years in combat, Van Deventer flew Spitfires with both the British and later with the US 52nd Fighter Group, P-38s with the 14th Fighter Group, and finally P-47s with the 373rd Fighter Group's 410th Fighter Squadron. His final tally was four confirmed kills, although he had scored two probable Ju 88 kills while with the British. His July 7, 1944, mission bagged his last two, a pair of Me 109s while over the Normandy beachhead:

"I was flying as Blue Leader at 24,000ft [7,315m] near Ouistreham at 1915hrs. I saw a dogfight at 10,000ft [3,048m] and called to drop tanks and engage. We dived at about 500mph [805kmh] and I saw an Me 109G break off and head southeast. I caught him on the deck and fired about a three-second burst at 50yd [46m] dead astern. He took no evasive action. The 109 poured white smoke and large explosions were

4A St. Louis Globe-Democrat. Friday, June 9, 1944

St. Louisan Downs 2 of 8 ME-109s Attacking 4 Mates, Runs Bag to 10

A St. Louis fighter pilot, Capt. Cowell Vandeventer, probably saved the lives of four fellow flyers who were getting the worst of a dogfight with eight Germans yesterday when he shot down two Messerschmitt 109s over the invasion beachhead, according to an Associated Press dispatch. The double kill brought Vandeventer's total to 10, including two in North Africa and four with the RCAF in Britain. He also has two "probables" to his credit.

Vandeventer, 21-year-old Thunderbolt pilot, who flew with the RAF in the battle of Britain, was leading a patrol at 24,000 feet when he spotted four Thunderbolts mixing with the Germans at 5000 feet.

"Our boys were getting the worst of it, too," he said. "I called over the radio, 'Take it easy; our flight is coming,' and flew down with my boys after me."

As one of the Germans broke off the fight and headed inland, Vandeventer gave chase and shot him down at a range of 50 yards, the dispatch said.

Ten miles away he spotted another ME109 at low altitude. By flying 100 feet above the ground Vandeventer got under the German and gave him a fatal burst.

Capt. Vandeventer is the nephew of Mrs. Maude O. Johnson, with whom he has made his home at 6028 Clemens avenue since the death of his parents. A former RCAF flyer, he transferred to the Army Air Forces after this country went to war. He is a graduate of Blewett High School and received his basic flying training at Lambert-St. Louis Field.

Left: Newspaper clipping reporting on Capt. Van Deventer's double-kill mission of June 7, 1944.

seen from the engine. Lt. Hamlet also fired at this plane and scored hits on both wings and tail. Lt. Hamlet and I saw him crash. We were then attacked by an Me 109 and I broke sharply to the left in a tight 360-degree turn and evidently lost him. Also, I lost Lt. Hamlet. I then saw a 109 hitting the deck about 7 or 8 miles [11 or 13km] to the south. I chased him for ten minutes. He was at about 300ft [91m] and I was dead astern and slightly below him. As he was making shallow five-degree weaves, I weaved with him so that he could not see me and he took no evasive action. I closed to 50ft [15m] and gave him a three-second burst. He poured white smoke and a large explosion came from the engine. He crashed into a stone wall and broke up.

John B. Hamlet, Van Deventer's wingman, stayed with his leader as they dove from altitude and got a good burst in at the 109 they were both chasing. "I was Blue 2 in Capt. Van Deventer's flight. After having dived from 24,000ft [7,315m] we closed in dead astern on an Me 109 on the deck. Capt. Van Deventer opened fire first, scoring hits on the wings and in the engine. Then I was able to get in a three-second burst and observed hits on the wings and tail section. Two seconds later, he crashed."

Lt. Jesse Harris, leading Van Deventer's second element, was having issues with getting his rounds on target: "While flying number three position on patrol with Blue Flight at 24,000ft [7,315m], Capt. Van Deventer spotted a dogfight at about 8,000ft [2,438m]. He ordered us to drop belly tanks and dive to the fight. We dove at approximately 500mph [805kmh]. I made several head-on passes at an Me 109 and a few very high deflection passes. My firing was very ineffective and when my ammunition was expended, I told my wingman Lt. Eichelberger to take over. He made several passes from smaller angles than I did. He hit the enemy aircraft and smoke streamed from it. It went into a gentle dive from about 300ft [91m] and crashed into the ground and burned. The fighting took place from 4,500ft [1,372m] down to 0ft and I expended 1,700 rounds of .50-caliber ammunition."

Lt. William Eichelberger was number four in the flight, covering Harris as he engaged the Messerschmitt: "We were patrolling over the beachhead at 24,000ft [7,315m] and Capt. Van Deventer, our Blue Flight

Above: Low over Mont St. Michel, this 410th Fighter Squadron razorback has had its invasion stripes overpainted recently, dating this photo to August 1944.

Above: Belted .50-caliber ammunition came in 350-round crates, each weighing about 100lb (45kg) fully loaded.

leader, saw the enemy aircraft below and ordered us to drop belly tanks. We did and went into a steep dive at about 500mph [805kmh]. Lt. Harris, my element leader, attacked one Me 109 at about 4,500ft [1,372m] and we made several head-on passes until he was out of ammunition. He then ordered me to take over. I attacked the 109 and fired a deflection burst of about 40 degrees from seven-thirty and got a few hits. The 109 then chopped his throttle and I had to kick right rudder hard to keep from crashing into him. He then gave it the throttle and started a tight left turn. I got in another deflection shot and black smoke began to pour from his engine. He then straightened out and I closed to about 75yd [69m] astern and gave him another burst and he exploded and crashed into the ground about 500ft [152m] below us"

Scarcely a month after his double-kill mission, Capt. Van Deventer was again leading his flight when his airplane was hit. Lt. Richard Nickerson had been separated from his flight and joined up with Van Deventer's just as they were entering the target area: "I was flying Yellow 4 and we came down to 5,000ft [1,524m] due to weather and saw flak ahead of us over Elbeuf. I broke left and was separated from Yellow Flight, so I joined Blue Flight which consisted of three aircraft. We went down to the deck and flew along a river valley heading south to Evereux at approximately 50ft [15m]. We got into considerable light flak from the airfield east of Evereux and we pulled up in a right climbing turn. Then I saw that Blue Leader had been hit in the tail and flames were visible.

"Immediately, he leveled off at about 200ft [61m], then nosed down and crashed in the woods south of Evereux with a very large explosion. After Blue Leader was hit, I saw smoke from two bomb bursts developing north of the highway, but I don't know if they were Blue Leader's bombs or not as there were other aircraft in the area."

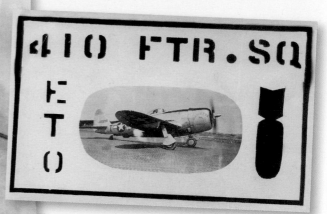

Above: "Marietta", a late-war P-47D from the 410th Fighter Squadron is taxiing out from Venlo, Holland in March or early April 1945. .
Left: A 411th Fighter Squadron ground crewman in Capt. Edward Miller's P-47 at LeCulot airfield, Belgium, early 1945.

Down and Dirty in the MTO

"As I broke away, two cannon shells hit my right wing, causing my right wheel to drop and set the wing on fire. I tried turning, but my ship was crippled. . . . I hit the deck, trying to evade his fire. Immediately two more Me 109s jumped me. The three of them ran a gunnery pattern on me from line abreast abeam. I took hits all over the aircraft."

—Capt. Al Froning, 65th Fighter Squadron, December 16, 1943

While the 8th Air Force introduced the P-47 to combat, the 9th and more specifically the 12th Air Force honed the Thunderbolt into a complete weapon system. In addition to new tactics, new engines and propellers greatly improved the Thunderbolt's performance at lower altitudes. The introduction of water injection on the R2800-21 engine gave a critical boost of on-demand power and broad-chord Hamilton Standard and later Curtiss Electric propellers greatly improved climb performance, probably the P-47's greatest weakness.

The first Thunderbolts in the Mediterranean were assigned to the strategic 15th Air Force's 325th Fighter Group for bomber escort duty. The group transitioned from the P-40F to the P-47D in October 1943, escorting 15th Air Force bombers to targets in northern Italy, Yugoslavia, and Austria over a period of seven months before their P-51s arrived in May. The 332nd Fighter Group's tenure with the Thunderbolt was even shorter, lasting only six weeks from May to June 1944.

The 12th Air Force was the first organization to adapt the P-47 as a fighter-bomber. Innovative commanders like Maj. Gil Wymond of the 65th Fighter Squadron sought to improve on the design in order to perform better at lower altitude. One of the major modifications made by

Left: Maj. Charles Gilbert was the CO of the 346th Fighter Squadron in the closing months of the war, leading the squadron in many of its critical missions against the Luftwaffe in northern Italy.

Wymond and one of his senior NCOs was to change the P-47 bomb-release system in the cockpit. The P-47D-15-RE and later variants came with wing pylons installed, but the release mechanisms for both wing pylons and the centerline hardpoint were all on the lower left side of the cockpit. This arrangement made dive-bombing exceedingly difficult, as the pilot had to divert his attention away from flying in order to look down, identify the proper bomb-release handle, and pull it. Wymond's solution was to move the release handles up to the bottom portion of the main control panels and rewire them from there. The procedure from there was simple: left hand off throttle and onto the control panel, slide down until contact is made with the three handles, and then pull the appropriate handle(s). The system was so effective that Republic standardized it on the production line.

By summer 1944, the P-47 was the standard fighter of the 12th Air Force, equipping six groups in two Tactical Air Commands (XII and XXII TAC), assigned to support the US Seventh and Fifth Armies respectively. When Seventh Army's VI Corps landed on the shores of southern France in August 1944, the majority of 12th Air Force Thunderbolts were in direct support of the ground forces. As Seventh Army pushed north and eastward, the Twelfth Air Force split its two TACs, XII TAC staying in France as part of the 1st Tactical Air Force (attached to the 9th Air Force) and XXII TAC remaining in Italy with Fifth Army.

Ace!- The 57th over Yugoslavia

The 57th Fighter Group was the first American fighter group to reach North Africa. Flying combat alongside the British from July 1942 onwards as part of the Desert Air Force (DAF), the 57th's pilots learned the value of effective close air support (CAS) as well as air superiority from their British counterparts.

With the 1943 reorganizations of the American air forces in the European-African-Middle Eastern Theater of Operations, the 57th was designated a fighter-bomber unit and would transfer to the 12th Air Force and transition from the P-40F to the P-47D by year's end.

The 57th arrived in Italy in September 1943 and began flying from Foggia on the eastern side of southern Italy. From Foggia, they were able to strike German targets in Yugoslavia, and by October the group's P-40s were striking targets across the Adriatic. With the group's transition to the Thunderbolt in November, the 57th's pilots gained increased time over Yugoslavian targets, an extra pair of .50-caliber machine guns, and a significant increase in the amount of ordnance carried. A month later, on December 16, 1943, the 57th met the Germans in the air for the first time.

Above: *Capt. Al Froning scored his last two kills over Yugoslavia on December 16, 1943, making him the 57th Fighter Group's last ace.*

German forces in Yugoslavia were a major concern, as they were on the dividing line between Eastern and Western Fronts. Fighters based there could intercept Allied bombers flying from Italy and were also in relatively close proximity to Soviet forces. As an extension of the POINTBLANK directive, 12th Air Force Thunderbolts were unleashed on German airfields across the Adriatic to take the pressure off of Allied forces on both fronts.

Lts. Alfred Froning and Harold Monohan both accounted for themselves well. Lt. Froning was "leading top flight of three P-47s. We had just pulled up from strafing [the target, nicknamed] 'stone' and were at 1,000ft [328m]. Lt. Monohan called in one snapper and attacked the same. As he dove on the enemy

Bottom left and right: Rockets—4.5in (114mm) fin-stabilized "Bazooka" rockets were a new weapon in the Thunderbolt's arsenal in spring 1944. Initial results with the triple rocket tubes were mixed, but as pilots gained experience with aiming and firing the projectiles, results improved significantly.

Below: The 15th Air Force began flying to Yugoslavia from bases in Italy in late 1943. Luftwaffe airfields and transportation there then became the primary targets of 12th Air Force P-47 strafers.

Meanwhile, Lt. Monohan was having similar success, shooting down a pair of Messerschmitts as well. "I was ordered off at 0800hrs on a strafing mission over Yugoslavia. Upon completion of our strafing attack, I and the other P-47s sighted 15-plus Me 109s. I attacked one flying on the deck, he did a chandelle [a 180-degree turn combined with a climb] up to the left, I followed shooting all the time. Smoke began to pour from him when about 400ft [122m] above the sea. Looking back, I saw him crash into the sea. I then sighted one on my left and did a 90-degree turn firing a long burst at close range. I then had to break off as another Me 109 was closing in on me. I turned into him, but did not engage. I then looked to my right and saw the 109 which I had previously engaged go down in smoke and crash, the pilot of which bailed out."

Although he narrowly escaped being shot down too, Alfred Froning scored his fifth and sixth kills on December 16, making him the first and only 57th Fighter Group pilot to become an ace in the P-47. As the mission focus shifted from destroying enemy aircraft to destroying enemy transportation and fuel, the 57th's opportunities to engage enemy aircraft dwindled, with the group scoring only nineteen kills in 1944 and a single in 1945. Yet the 57th, along with the 79th and 350th Fighter Groups, provided essential air cover for Fifth Army and continued the even more crucial destruction of enemy fuel and transportation in northern Italy.

aircraft, another Me 109 closed in on his tail. I was above and behind and closed in for a dead astern shot at a 250yd [229m] range. I opened fire and observed pieces and smoke trail off this 109. He tried to pull up and I continued firing. He then half rolled at 900ft [274m] and went straight into the water, burning. As I broke away, two cannon shells hit my right wing, causing my right wheel to drop and set the wing on fire. I tried turning, but my ship was crippled resulting in my tail getting shot up. I hit the deck, trying to evade his fire. Immediately two more Me 109s jumped me. The three of them ran a gunnery pattern on me from line abreast abeam. I took hits all over the aircraft. Two of the 109s left, the remaining ship turned on the tail of another P-47 that crossed our path. I turned about and fired a 30-degree deflection shot gradually closing it down to line astern. I observed approximately 3 or 4ft [0.9 or 1.2m] of his left wing fly off and the balance of his tail sections. He was throwing much black and white smoke. He was at 400ft [122m] and started to roll over on his back in a 60-degree dive. When last seen he was at 150ft [46m] apparently out of control on his back, smoking before he crashed into the sea."

Above: Mud was a constant issue in the spring of 1944 and hampered 12th Air Force fighter-bomber sorties as a result.

Surprise Attack!

USAAF intelligence had been intercepting Luftwaffe communications for several weeks after 15th Air Force operations began and, after careful analysis, patterns to the German units' behavior began to emerge. The situations under which the Luftwaffe scrambled fighters to intercept the bomber formations became clearer, and on January 30, 1944, the 325th Fighter Group intended to catch the Germans either still on the ground or just taking off to intercept. The heavies were dispatched to hit the airfield complex around Villaorba and Udine, which lay between American airfields in Italy and strategic targets in Austria and Germany.

Sixty P-47s took off at 0945hrs and, according to group intelligence officer, Capt. Ken Setterdahl, "flew a course of 350-degrees for 75 miles [121km] at an altitude between 5 and 50ft [1.5 to 15m] above the water." The three squadron leaders flew on instruments while their

Above: *Maj. Herschel "Herky" Green became an "ace in a day" on January 30, 1944, when he shot down six German aircraft.*

squadrons followed visually, maintaining a tight formation. "Turning to a heading of 333-degrees, they then flew another 225 miles [362km] at an altitude so low that their prop wash was leaving visible wakes in the water behind them. It was a hazy day and distinguishing sea from sky was almost impossible." One break in concentration by any of the squadron leaders could mean the entire group flying right into the Adriatic at more than 300mph [483kmh].

Capt. Herschel Green was leading the 317th Fighter Squadron on the two-hour flight and had his most successful day on the 30th. "When we made landfall on the north coast and started our climb, I was drenched with perspiration and absolutely exhausted physically and mentally. We arrived over the airfield complex at 1145hrs at 20,000ft [6,095m].

"Immediately upon leveling off and starting a turn to sweep the area, I spotted a number of large aircraft in a loose gaggle formation flying at very low altitude approaching one of the airfields. I pushed the nose of my Jug over and started down with my flight of four, leaving the remainder at altitude.

"The planes were Ju 52 transports flying at 1,000ft [305m]. I started down the line. As I exploded the last aircraft in the string, I switched to the next plane, got off a quick burst, setting it afire, and then switched to another, followed by a fourth, all with the same fatal results." As Green pulled into the vertical and around to make another pass, the rest of his flight, consisting of Cecil Dean, George Novotny, and Edsel Paulk, shot down the remaining Ju 52s, for a total of eleven. Yet things were just getting started.

Green sighted an Italian Macchi 202 diving in the opposite direction and turned to pull in on its tail, just above the ground. "The 202 after

Left: *The 325th "Checkertail Clan" was one of only two fighter groups to use the Thunderbolt in the high-altitude escort role in the Mediterranean Theater. The 325th operated the Jug from October 1943 through May 1944.*

Above: *"Focke Wulf," from the 319th Fighter Squadron was just one of the many adopted mascots of US fighter squadrons. Dogs were a great boost to morale.*

Right: *The jacket of Capt. Harold Wolfe, who joined the 325th Fighter Group's 317th Fighter Squadron in early 1944*

Brief But Effective – the 332nd Fighter Group

Usually when the Tuskeegee Airmen's contribution to the air war effort is discussed it focuses on the group's time flying the P-51. Reality is somewhat more complicated, and the 332nd's squadrons flew not only P-40s and P-51s, but P-39s and P-47s as well. The 332nd began combat operations with the P-47 in early June 1944 and on the 9th, the 301st and 302nd Fighter Squadrons scored their first kills against the Axis in their new mounts. On June 25, the 100th, 301st, and 302nd Fighter Squadrons were sent to strafe troop concentrations on two different roads in northeastern Italy and western Yugoslavia. Unable to find their primary target, eight Thunderbolts turned toward Trieste harbor and caught a German torpedo boat underway. The German vessel TA22 (formerly the Italian *Giuseppe Missori*) was a World War I-vintage torpedo boat, roughly the size of a US destroyer escort. The first pass was made by a two-ship formation consisting of Lt. Gwynne Pierson and Lt. Wendell Pruitt, who had just come out of a cloud bank and found themselves face-to-face with the vessel. The formation's P-47s were not carrying bombs, and so .50-caliber machine guns were the only available weapons. The rest of the formation followed, and after Pierson and Pruitt's rounds found their marks, the ship turned violently, but exposing the ship's flanks to repeated attacks by the Thunderbolts. During the attack, rounds hit and detonated the ship's magazine, reducing it to a smoking hulk. This would be the last significant action that the 332nd fought in the P-47, as their P-51 transition and their escort missions into Germany would begin just a few days later.

flying straight and level for about a minute, rolled into a tight 360-degree turn and then straightened out. I followed him in the turn and managed to gain a couple hundred feet of altitude on him, which I converted to additional speed by slowly bleeding it off. When he started a third turn, I was in range and let him have it. I saw multiple flashes all around the cockpit. The pilot must have been hit, for the airplane executed a perfect snap-roll at that extremely low altitude, coming back into almost level flight before the right wing dropped slowly into the ground and the 202 cartwheeled away in a ball of fire."

Alone by this time, Green turned for home, but spotted a lone Do 217 and dove in to attack. "As I climbed through 15,000ft [4,571m] heading south, I saw a twin-engine plane about 5,000ft [1,523m] below and behind me. I throttled back and began an easy, descending right turn so I would come down on his tail. When I opened fire, I saw hits on his left engine, which started to burn uncontrollably. I also saw tracers come from my guns. I pulled off and watched the Do 217 to see what would happen. It crash landed and exploded on impact."

Green's flight of four shot down sixteen airplanes for no losses and Green was awarded the Distinguished Service Cross for his six-kill mission. The group's tally for the day was thirty-four kills, which earned the 325th Fighter Group its second Distinguished Unit Citation.

Rescue in the Adriatic

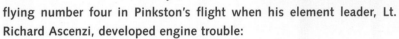

Winter weather over the Adriatic Sea was seldom pleasant. While ditching at sea was not as immediately life threatening as it would be in the English Channel in February, it was still an ominous prospect to face. With weather conditions worsening and the target area obscured by clouds, Col. Gladwyn Pinkston, CO of the 79th Fighter Group, turned his formation for home. First Lt. Irvin Grandjean was **flying number four in Pinkston's flight when his element leader, Lt. Richard Ascenzi, developed engine trouble:**

"On the morning of February 9, 1945, I was flying wing on Lt. Ascenzi on a 16-ship show which was heading south over the coast of the Adriatic at 10,000ft [3,048m], after abandoning our mission. Lt. Ascenzi was element leader in the four-ship lead flight led by Col. Pinkston. The colonel's wingman was Lt. Hearne. Just after our 180-degree turn (due to bad weather over the target area), Lt. Ascenzi dropped back out of position in the flight, calling over the R/T that he had loss of power. I throttled back and made S turns over him while he attempted to remedy the trouble. Both of us fell way back while Col. Pinkston and his wingman continued on course. I had made R/T contact with Lt. Ascenzi, telling him I would follow him. He then glided down in a rather steep angle into the heavy overcast at 8,000ft [2,438m], which immediately swallowed him up. I went in behind him, asking his altitude and position. He replied he had flown straight and broke through at 6,000ft [1,829m] and had no chance of regaining power and would jump at 1,000ft [328m]. Visibility was very poor beneath the top overcast. Scattered and broken clouds extended intermittently all the way to the water. Due to this fact, I was unable to sight Lt. Ascenzi in this very short period from the time he went into the top overcast until he jumped. I assumed we were some 20 to 30 miles [32 to 48km] off the coast southwest of Udine. It was then about 0815hrs. For the first five or ten minutes I searched for Lt. Ascenzi without definite pattern at 300 to 500ft [91 to 152m] above the sea. I had not set up a pattern as I had kept what I considered a close estimate of his jumping point.

"As soon as he first called that he was in trouble, I had flipped my IFF [Identification Friend or Foe system] on to position number three (emergency), went on Channel B on the VHF, and called "Commander" (shore control) to get a fix on my position. So far, the first ten minutes I flew in tight circles and figure eights expecting to see him immediately. It soon became evident that visibility was so badly restricted I could easily

Left: "Deacon Dandy" of the 86th Fighter Squadron waits for its next mission over Italy.

miss him though quite close to him. Scattered clouds at times came right to the surface of the sea, which fortunately was quite calm. I then set up a rectangular pattern with timed legs and proceeded to comb the area systematically. From time to time I was in radio contact with Maj. Zilly who remained in the general area for a while attempting to locate me. Bad weather prevented his doing so—he returned to base after the attempt. Also, he had R/T contact at one point with a British flight who relayed messages to Commander and back. Due to my low altitude, I could not talk to Commander directly. I was informed after about forty minutes of search to give up and return to base, as "Big Friends" would soon arrive to take over. However as I had sufficient gas, I remained and after about ten additional minutes, sighted a green sea marker and finally the yellow dinghy. Lt. Ascenzi responded to my dive and wing rocking with vigorous arm waving. I climbed to 6,500ft [1,981m] keeping his location orbited as well as possible in the succeeding cloud layer and got a fix through to Commander. They instructed me to continue my orbiting until two Spitfires arrived. This I did, passing on the dinghy's location to them. The Spitfires began a low-altitude search. I was later joined by Col. Pinkston and the two of us went down again to the deck and took up the pattern. I was soon forced to return home because of gas shortage, with instructions to send out another pilot to join the colonel. However, on the trip home, Commander announced that the Spits had relocated the pilot in the dinghy and told the colonel to return home as "Big Friends" would complete the rescue. On my way home, I acted as relay for many messages both ways. I landed at about 1110hrs after four hours and five minutes in the air."

The Air-Sea Rescue network in Italy was very similar to the established system in England, although there was no dedicated P-47-equipped Emergency Rescue Squadron to loiter over downed pilots and drop supplies. Pilots in the Mediterranean Theater relied on one another to radio in the position to their ground controllers and then ASR, should one of them go down over water. As with all fighter pilots, the downed aviator's wingman would remain on station until relieved or the one "in the drink" was picked up by a British ASR boat or an RAF or USAAF "Dumbo" flying boat.

Below: The "Pocket Guide to North Africa" would bring US personnel up to speed on local culture and geography.

Below and bottom: The .50-caliber linking machine was an essential tool for P-47 armorers. Each ammunition crate held 350 rounds and each gun had an ammunition capacity of 475 rounds. The linking machine enabled armorers to link belts together without tearing up their fingers.

POCKET GUIDE TO
NORTH AFRICA

Above: A newly issued 79th Fighter Group P-47D-30-RE undergoing maintenance checks prior to being issued to one of the group's three squadrons

Rover Joe and Horsefly — In-Theater Fighter Control

"As he enters the room, there are two loudspeakers (LS-10) to be seen, each with telephones hooked up. These speakers and phones are the heart of air–ground cooperation. Those are the things you must have in working order if you expect to talk to the pilots of those P-47s miles away from here, and steer them to targets, or get flash reports from them."

—XIX TAC Signals unit history

While the mission briefing, (whether hasty or deliberate) was the guideline for all Thunderbolt pilots on a mission, communication was critical whether on escort duty or bombing ground targets. Upon clearing its friendly airfield's airspace, the flight would be directed to contact the local controller, usually identified by an obscure two-syllable callsign that belied the importance of its mission. Once in contact, a controller like "Grubstake" (82nd Fighter Control Squadron, 12th Air Force) would relay mission instructions; that first controller contact could also be at the corps level, who would then push the flight down to a more local controller who had a better idea of the ground situation. These forward controllers were usually pilots assigned to frontline units along with a jeep, radio set, and a driver. By assigning pilots as "Rover Joes," the USAAF ensured a common language and thus far better communication between air and ground elements.

The XIX TAC Signals unit history paints a vivid picture of the many moving parts of the air–ground liaison team talking a flight of Thunderbolts onto a target and how the speed of radio communication with those P-47s can often outpace the speed of the operations office:

"Maj. Iverson, the XII Corps Tactical Liaison Officer (TALO) scurries into the office after an early breakfast. As he enters the room, there are two loudspeakers (LS-10) to be seen, each with telephones hooked up. These speakers and phones are the heart of air–ground cooperation. Those are the things you must have in working order if you expect to talk

Above: *The Stinson L-5 Sentinel proved to be the ideal platform for "Horsefly" forward air controllers. It was faster and more robust than the Piper L-4.*

to the pilots of those P-47s miles away from here, and steer them to targets, or get flash reports from them. When the VHF sets at a division are out, you may as well forget about close cooperation until you get them fixed, so completely does air cooperation depend on good communications.

Left: *Maj. Thomas Iverson served as a Tactical Air Liaison Officer for XII Corps, part of 3rd Army and coordinated XIX TAC P-47 units in support of General Patton's advance across Europe.*

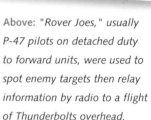

Above: *"Rover Joes," usually P-47 pilots on detached duty to forward units, were used to spot enemy targets then relay information by radio to a flight of Thunderbolts overhead.*

"This phone and speaker arrangement is the remote control for two VHF radios located about a mile from the CP [Command Post]. These sets are sited atop the tallest hill in the neighborhood and use 60ft [18m] antenna masts to get the best possible results. One radio is on the fighter-bomber channel, while the other is on the Tac Recce channel. In addition to the VHF rigs, an SCR-399 is also set up nearby in contact with all parties at each division and with the NCS at XIX TAC. The setup at division is similar, except that only one VHF set (for fighter-bomber work) is in operation. When the division isn't getting any 'air,' the TALO will switch to the Tac Recce channel to pick up Recce flashes.

"Maj. Iverson, the TALO, does most of his work with Col. Strong, the G-3 Air. The major is a qualified pilot and hit the coast of France as a TALO with the 79th Division. He controls the fighter-bombers in the area. He knows good targets from bad. It's up to him and the G-3 Air to decide which division in the corps will get air in the next five or ten minutes."

Always the innovators when it came to P-47 operations, the 12th Air Force took the process one step further. Installing the SCR-522 VHF radio set in an L-5 spotter plane, the 12th's Thunderbolt pilots rotated through frontline service on six week tours in order to fly as "Horsefly" forward air controllers. The one major drawback with Rover Joes was that pilots on the ground did not have the luxury of seeing the target as the inbound Thunderbolts would. By putting another pilot in the air with a low and slow view of the battlefield over the frontlines, Horsefly could then talk an incoming flight of Thunderbolts onto a target far more effectively.

Cutting Off the Escape

As German forces withdrew northwards out of Italy in the closing days of the war, the Po River remained their last obstacle before reaching the relative safety of the Alps. In the last two weeks of the war, Thunderbolt fighter-bombers braved withering AAA fire to destroy as many pieces of enemy war materiel as possible before the Germans crossed the Po, from where they would be able to continue the war effort. On April 23, 1945, 346th Fighter Squadron commander Maj. Charles Gilbert led a four-ship strafing mission against one of these troop and vehicle concentrations waiting to cross the Po. "I took my section to Sermide and found the roads and fields filled with enemy equipment. We split up into two elements and started to work. The flak was so intense that I ordered the flight to drop their belly tanks. I found ten–fifteen big trucks and trailers in a field south of Sermide and Lt. Domin and I started making scissoring passes on them. As I pulled off my fifth pass, I saw Lt. Domin pulling up to the west, on fire. I ordered him to bail out. I repeated the order twice more before I saw the plane turn over on its back to the left and go in. At the same time, I saw Lt. Domin's chute open at about 1,200ft [366m]. He seemed to be OK. The flak was still intense but there was no plane within ¾ mile [1.2km] of him. By the time I got over to him, he was touching the ground. When he hit, he was either dead or unconscious. I buzzed him once and saw his chute had collapsed after dragging him about 15 or 20ft [4.5 to 6m]. Lt. Domin just lay there. This was in an open field about 6 miles [10km] south of Sermide. Yellow 3 and 4 buzzed him three or four times while I covered them."

First Lieutenant Ray Knight, one of the most aggressive pilots in the 346th Fighter Squadron, was flying as Yellow Three in Maj. Gilbert's flight: "We took off and proceeded to the vicinity of Sermide, where much motor transport had been reported to us by Minefield Green Flight who were already there. Arriving, we began to strafe the trucks, we separated into two-ship elements and picked out our targets. After a few minutes, Maj. Gilbert spotted a large concentration of transports in an open field and called me to come

Above: *Lt. Ray Knight.*

over and help strafe it. As I approached the field, I saw Lt. Domin pulling up from a strafing pass on the motor transports, he pulled up and turned to the left and I observed intense light flak being fired at him. At about 2,000ft [610m], his plane burst into flames and I heard Maj. Gilbert call him and tell him to bail out as he was on fire. His plane rolled over on its back and at about 1,200ft [366m], he bailed out. I saw his chute open and watched him float down. On the way down in his chute, I observed flak being fired at him and bursting all around him. When he hit the ground, he made no attempt to spill his chute or move in any manner. The chute dragged him about 20ft [6m] before collapsing. I then saw about six Jerry soldiers come out and look at him a few minutes and then walk off. He had landed in a plowed field about 30ft [9m] off a road running east and west just southwest of Sermide. I then buzzed him three times. He was lying face down and his head appeared to be missing. There was a large spot of blood around his head, or where his head should have been. I then left this area to join up with Maj. Gilbert. I flew back over the spot about five minutes later to see if Lt. Domin had moved, but he was gone then. I think some Italians from a house nearby had moved him."

Above: *Maj. Gilbert's "Torrid Tessie" is armed with two 110-gal (416-liter) napalm tanks. Napalm came into use in mid-1944, P-47s being the first to use it.*

1st Lt. Ray Knight—Medal of Honor

Lt. Knight *(below)* was back in the air again on April 24, 1945, this time to Ghedi airdrome, and the following day over Bergamo airdrome. His fearless leadership over these two days earned him the final Medal of Honor awarded to an airman in World War II. His citation reads:

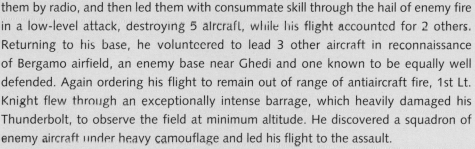

"He piloted a fighter-bomber aircraft in a series of low-level strafing missions, destroying 14 grounded enemy aircraft and leading attacks which wrecked 10 others during a critical period of the Allied drive in northern Italy. On the morning of 24 April, he volunteered to lead 2 other aircraft against the strongly defended enemy airdrome at Ghedi. Ordering his fellow pilots to remain aloft, he skimmed the ground through a deadly curtain of antiaircraft fire to reconnoiter the field, locating 8 German aircraft hidden beneath heavy camouflage. He rejoined his flight, briefed them by radio, and then led them with consummate skill through the hail of enemy fire in a low-level attack, destroying 5 aircraft, while his flight accounted for 2 others. Returning to his base, he volunteered to lead 3 other aircraft in reconnaissance of Bergamo airfield, an enemy base near Ghedi and one known to be equally well defended. Again ordering his flight to remain out of range of antiaircraft fire, 1st Lt. Knight flew through an exceptionally intense barrage, which heavily damaged his Thunderbolt, to observe the field at minimum altitude. He discovered a squadron of enemy aircraft under heavy camouflage and led his flight to the assault.

"Returning alone after this strafing, he made 10 deliberate passes against the field despite being hit by antiaircraft fire twice more, destroying 6 fully loaded enemy twin-engine aircraft and 2 fighters. His skillfully led attack enabled his flight to destroy 4 other twin-engine aircraft and a fighter plane. He then returned to his base in his seriously damaged plane. Early the next morning, when he again attacked Bergamo, he sighted an enemy plane on the runway. Again he led 3 other American pilots in a blistering low-level sweep through vicious antiaircraft fire that damaged his plane so severely that it was virtually non-flyable. Three of the few remaining enemy twin-engine aircraft at that base were destroyed. Realizing the critical need for aircraft in his unit, he declined to parachute to safety over friendly territory and unhesitatingly attempted to return his shattered plane to his home field. With great skill and strength, he flew homeward until caught by treacherous air conditions in the Appennines Mountains [sic], where he crashed and was killed. The gallant action of 1st Lt. Knight eliminated the German aircraft which were poised to wreak havoc on Allied forces pressing to establish the first firm bridgehead across the Po River; his fearless daring and voluntary self-sacrifice averted possible heavy casualties among ground forces and the resultant slowing on the German drive culminated in the collapse of enemy resistance in Italy."

Typical attire of a 9th or 12th Air Force Thunderbolt pilot in spring 1945.

Covering the Advance

"Three of the four 190s turned and headed east. The fourth remained on my tail and I immediately began a Lufberry to the right. Evidently this enemy pilot was inexperienced for after two turns, I got on his tail and put a burst into his fuselage. Instantly, he did a half-snap roll and went straight in, exploding violently as he crashed."

—1st Lt. Talmadge Ambrose, on his Distinguished Service Cross (DSC) mission, April 8, 1945

The Allied landings in Normandy brought the P-47's air war down to lower altitudes. While the Thunderbolt had traditionally been a high-altitude fighter, upgrades in tactics, airframe, engine, and propeller had evolved the P-47 into the most potent American fighter-bomber of the war. With Allied armies advancing slowly but steadily through Normandy in 1944, the Jug's massive firepower was often the decisive edge that American ground units held over the Germans.

The 8th Air Force continued to fly from England, but by mid-July the 9th began flying from advanced bases in Normandy close to the frontlines, shortening refuel/rearm times and enabling "Thunderbombers" to get back into the fight quickly in order to support troops better on the ground. As the Allied armies gained ground on the continent, the 9th's fighter-bombers were forced to keep pace, with most 9th Air Force groups switching airfields two or three times in the autumn of 1944.

The 9th Air Force's Fighter Command (9th FC) steadily grew in strength, so that by the end of December all but one 8th Air Force group had converted to the P-51 and transferred their Thunderbolts to the 9th, which now boasted nearly 1,200 Thunderbolts in fifteen groups. The 9th FC's four Tactical Air Commands (TACs)—IX, XIX,

Left: 36th Fighter Group Thunderbolts taxi at Le Culot airfield in Belgium. Minutes after takeoff, they would be over German lines, beating back the German 5th and 6th SS Panzer Armies.

XXIX, and XII TAC—were each tasked with supporting one of the four US field armies (First, Third, Ninth, and Seventh Army respectively) as they fought eastward. XII TAC had originally been part of the Italy-based 12th Air Force, but was split off and attached to the 9th Air Force when Seventh Army landed in southern France that August, adding another 240 combat-ready airplanes.

The summer of 1944 also saw the introduction of two major upgrades. First was the introduction of new broad-chord propellers on the P-47D-22 and 23 models. The P-47D-22-RE used the Hamilton Standard 13ft (4m) 24E50-65 propeller, while the P-47D-23-RA built in Evansville, Indiana, used the Curtiss Electric C542S 13ft (4m) prop. Both propellers were better able to apply the additional power given by water injection in the newer versions of the R2800 engine, and they significantly increased the Thunderbolt's rate of climb.

The other upgrade drastically changed the Jug's appearance. The P-47D-25-RE, introduced a cut-down aft fuselage and a clear Perspex "bubble" canopy, which offered far better pilot visibility, particularly downward and to the rear, although some lateral stability was sacrificed. Hand-me-down airplanes from the converting 8th Air Force groups were the norm as the 9th Air Force began flying combat missions over the continent, and it was not until late fall 1944 that the new "bubbletops" began arriving at 9th Air Force frontline units in large numbers.

Dogfight with Focke-Wulfs

By mid-July 1944, the frontlines in Western Europe had stagnated and the Allies were still contained within Normandy. It was clear that air power would be an essential component if the US First Army was to break out of the hedgerows and into the more open country near Paris. As the front shifted and airfields were liberated, 9th Air Force fighter groups began the move across the English Channel.

During that week, the 365th Fighter Squadron focused its dive-bombing missions around Chartres, interdicting rail lines, gun emplacements, and fuel dumps. On the 14th, Capt. Jack Coulter's formation of eight P-47s was inbound to their target when they sighted a large formation of enemy aircraft near Dreux:

"I was leading Sherwood White Flight at 2,500ft [762m], 1,000ft [305m] below the overcast. Three Fw 190s came out of the overcast at 11 o'clock and I called to the flight to drop bombs and belly tanks. Immediately after, twenty-plus Fw 190s and Me 109s broke out of the clouds behind the first three enemy aircraft. I continued on course, letting these pass over as they did not seem to observe us. Then about twenty more enemy aircraft following the first two formations broke down and behind us and we broke left into them. I fired on one from

put me on the Me 109's tail. He turned about 90 degrees and I was firing on him all the time with about 30 degrees deflection. Then he straightened out and entered the overcast. I was then firing from dead astern and observed strikes on his wings and fuselage. I winged over out of the overcast and saw him come spinning down off my right wing, crashing into the ground and burning. I saw no chute. I then found myself on another 109's tail and started firing with about 25–30 degrees deflection, when I observed my tracers coming out. I fired two more short bursts when an Fw 190 came in from 90 degrees closing to about 30 degrees firing on me. I racked it in hard, pulling into the overcast and lost him. I broke back down below the overcast to try to pick up the rest of my flight but saw nothing except enemy aircraft."

Coulter's wingman, 2nd Lt. Donald Childs, confirmed his flight leader's kill and scored one of his own: "I was flying Sherwood White Two when I noticed a flight of three Me 109s at 11 o'clock low in a V formation. My radio receiver was out and I tried to call my flight leader's attention to these when I saw him jettison his bombs and belly tank. I dropped my bombs safe and tried to get rid of my belly tank, but by this time the flight had started a sharp break to the left and I saw two Me 109s coming in from 5 o'clock high. This was the last I saw of Sherwood White Three and Four. I slid in under my flight leader, made one 360-degree turn, and had started another when he started shooting at an Me 109. I observed strikes and fire before the enemy aircraft went into the overcast. Capt. Coulter fired on into the overcast and I then saw the enemy aircraft come out of the overcast on fire and when last seen was going in at a 60-degree dive about 300ft [91m] from the ground. I broke left with two Me 109s shooting at me with about 45 degrees deflection. I zoomed into the overcast and then came back down looking for my flight leader when I saw an Me 109 at about 800yd [732m] turning left. I gave him a short burst but didn't have a large enough lead, he broke into the overcast and I lost him. I stayed in my left turn and I saw two Fw 190s shooting at a lone P-47. I called for him to break left and as he did, they slid past his tail. At this time I noticed two Me 109s crawling up on me with the inside man shooting tracers over my left wing. I broke down and to the left on

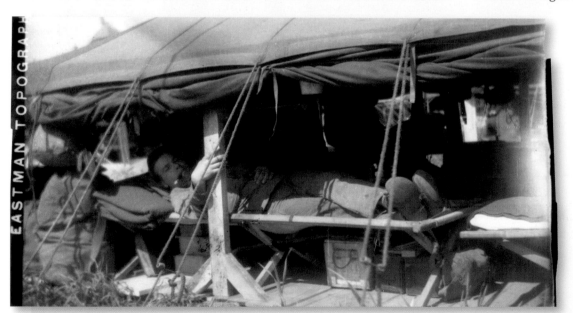

Above: *365th Fighter Squadron crew chief Sgt. Orrin Buffington takes a break on his cot during a moment of down time.*

about 30 degrees deflection, but observed no strikes before it entered the clouds. I then broke down and left and saw an Fw 190 on a silver P-47's tail. The 190 was getting strikes on the left wing and fuselage of the P-47. I broke into them and both enemy planes broke right, which a lone Me 109. I opened fire and pushed on water injection. I had started to close when he rolled out and started up for the overcast. I observed strikes on his wing roots and I continued to fire into the overcast. I broke clear between two layers and saw a plane go down in flames and hit the ground just off my left wing. I then pulled on into the overcast and broke out on top. Seeing no planes anywhere, I set course for base."

Right: The A-11 flight helmet became the standard for US fighter pilots by early 1944.

Red Flight's Charles Kern came out of the overcast and was unable to locate his flight so he joined up with Coulter: "I followed White Leader through his first break and then broke toward a 190 coming in from the right. He broke off and made a diving turn to the right and I got a short burst at 90 degrees deflection before he disappeared into a cloud. I then looked around for the rest of the flight and saw one P-47 off to my left. I got in trail with him to cover his tail and then someone yelled break and I broke hard left and saw two Fw 190s slide past my tail. They didn't seem to be able to turn with me and I maneuvered to a position of about 30 to 40 degrees deflection on one of them and got about a three-second burst at that angle. I was pretty sure I was hitting them although I could not decide whether it was smoke or cloud wisps that I saw coming from him. Just as he entered a cloud, he fell off badly on a wing and this is the one I claim as a probable. I couldn't follow him through the clouds to see if I had definitely gotten him as I had to break into a couple more who were coming at me. I got in a few more snap shots at various other planes when they popped out of the overcast, observing no results. I don't remember just how many planes I shot at in all. I circled for a while trying

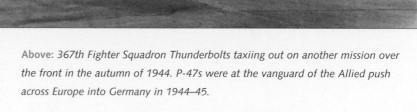

Above: 367th Fighter Squadron Thunderbolts taxiing out on another mission over the front in the autumn of 1944. P-47s were at the vanguard of the Allied push across Europe into Germany in 1944–45.

to locate another P-47 to join up on, but could not find any kind of planes at all, either friendly or enemy. I then decided it would be best to head for home, so I took my heading home and flew partially in the overcast.

Flying Top Cover

After the Allies' Normandy breakout in July 1944, and their invasion of southern France in August, the German Army had been pushed all the way back to the German border. The 371st Fighter Group had been with the 9th Air Force since England and was one of several 9th groups transferred to the XII TAC to increase the P-47 presence over Seventh Army. The group's 406th Fighter Squadron was en route to hit the marshaling yard at Karlsruhe on October 3, when 1st Lt. Forrest Kilgore's flight dove in to protect the bomb-laden P-47s of Red and Yellow Flights: "The squadron was going northeast to dive-bomb the railway lines near Karlsruhe. I was leading Blue Flight of three as cover at 12,500ft [3,810m]. At Rupt Sur Marne, I saw twenty-four Me 109s going southwest at 2 o'clock to us at 15,000ft [4,572m]. They dropped their belly tanks and proceeded to 5 o'clock. Sixteen made a pass at my flight. We turned into them. Their first flight scored hits on my plane and my number-three man. I fired a burst at their last flight, but did not observe any hits.

Above: Lt. Rudy Augarten scored against a pair of Me 109s on October 3, 1944, but ironically later flew a 109 in Israeli service four years later.

Left: Sgt. Harry Nickel (center, bottom row) served as a 406th FS crew chief from June 1944.
Below: The 371st used older 8th Air Force Thunderbolts that had been exchanged for P-51s.

"My engine was acting up, so I dropped my nose in a dive and opened my canopy. When I applied water injection the engine caught on again and I began a pass on a 109 in close pursuit of a P-47. He snap rolled and spiraled down to about 6,000ft [1,829m]. I followed him in a split-S and was able to get in a short burst from 300yd [274m] as he zoomed up again. He hammerhead stalled [pulled up into the vertical until his airspeed was zero] and I was able to fire a fairly long burst from about 250yd [229m] away. His plane seemed to go out of control. It leveled out momentarily and I fired a short burst closing from 250 to 100yd [229 to 91m] and overshot him. I turned and saw him pull up abruptly with blue smoke coming from his engine and then split-S straight into the ground where the plane burned."

His wingman, 2nd Lt. Rudy Augarten, would down two Messerschmitts on this mission and would go on to become an ace in the skies over Israel four years later: "I was flying Blue Two, the cover flight, when we sighted twenty-plus bogies about 3,000ft [914m] above us at 2 o'clock. We were at 12,500ft [3,810m]. We started a gradual turn into them to identify them. They turned into the sun. I identified them as Me 109s and called them out as such over the radio. The lead flight bounced Blue Flight. I broke and observed many planes milling around south of me. I bounced a lone 109. He kept in a turn to the left, and I stayed behind

him, firing about six bursts from 350 to 400yd [320 to 366m]. They were falling short. I increased my deflection and saw strikes on his left wing and left side of the fuselage. He rolled out of the turn in about a 40-degree dive, smoking. I continued to fire from close range and saw his canopy open and pieces fly off the plane. I pulled up at 6,000ft [1,829m] and lost him under my wing as I turned. Then I saw a parachute about 3,000ft [914m] below and a fire where the plane had hit the ground.

"I then headed climbing toward Belfort where I saw about twelve planes in a dogfight above the town. I was at about 11,000ft [3,353m]. About 1,000ft [305m] below me, a lone 109 was circling counterclockwise around the town. I closed in to about 350yd [320m] and fired several bursts. The second burst hit him. The plane smoked and rolled out in a slight dive. I closed to about 70yd [64m] and his glycol blew up, filling my cockpit with fumes. I pulled up and saw him bail out. I took camera pictures of his chute. Then I called Yearling leader and he said to rendezvous west of Belfort. I rejoined the squadron and returned to base with them."

2nd Lt. Lawrence Damewood was flying the position of Blue Three: "Our flight was jumped first and I became separated from the other two planes in the flight. I pulled up to gain altitude and sighted a plane at about 11 o'clock to me. I thought it was one of our own boys and I started over to join on his wing. When I got within 1,000yd [914m] of him, I recognized him as an enemy plane. I attacked him from 5 o'clock as he turned to the left and I closed to about 300yd [274m] and fired a burst at him. I did not see any strikes. I continued on and noticed another 47 in the scramble behind me. I closed to within 100yd [91m] [of the enemy fighter] and I could see him in the cockpit with the canopy thrown off. I was lower than he and I could not fire. He did a half roll and I rolled with him and fired, observing hits on his tail and right wing. He continued going down, doing a vertical roll along the way. He went through some flak and I followed and my plane was hit in the engine—I kept with him. He pulled up in a steep climb and I followed, losing a little distance. I was 200yd [183m]

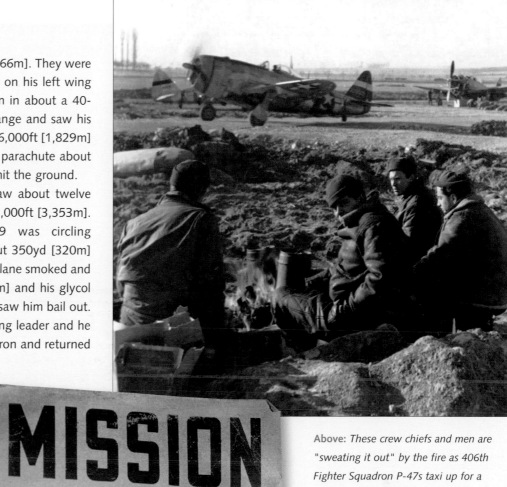

Above: *These crew chiefs and men are "sweating it out" by the fire as 406th Fighter Squadron P-47s taxi up for a take-off on a bombing mission.*
Left: *Each of the 9th Air Force's three TACs issued a brief commemorative history of the command's time in combat.*

away and he turned to the left, leveling out. I got in a good long burst, observing hits around the cockpit, on the fuselage and on the right wing. He started down. I saw the Jerry falling and strike the ground just north of Belfort. I pulled up and saw a plane on my right. It was Lt. Bailey. My engine started smoking and cut out. I bailed out near Plancher-des-Mines about 20 miles [32km] northwest of Belfort. I believe it was the flak which caused the damage to my engine."

Bridgehead Battles and V-1 Killers

The second week of March 1945 found the 492nd Fighter Squadron providing close support for the 9th Infantry Division around the Remagen bridgehead. On March 14, they flew three missions in support of 9th Division elements, with Maj. Norman Orwat leading the day's last mission that afternoon. Directed to a smoke-marked target by the "Cockspur" ground controller, Orwat's formation was starting its bomb run when they were diverted by a pair of Mustangs with a higher-priority target: "I was leading the squadron of eight aircraft on a dive-bombing mission when I was picked up by a P-51 [F-6] looking to show me a target. I made a radio call over "C" channel and the P-51 had us follow him to a concentration of ten tanks due east of the Remagen bridgehead—we had just started diving for the staging area when I observed 20–25 enemy aircraft starting down on us from 5 o'clock high. They came from atop a thin layer of stratus which was about 11,000ft [3,353m].

"I immediately switched channels and called for bombs to be jettisoned and a break to be made. Most of the enemy aircraft went through the formation, but three Me 109s singled me out and we entered a right-hand orbit. My wingman caused me to break off and I was finally able to get a deflection shot at another by pulling up into a steep chandelle [a 180-degree turn combined with a climb]. Since I had to pull almost straight up to get this shot, I stalled out completely. By the time I recovered, the 109 was going east, too far ahead of me to chase, and although I had observed strikes around his engine, they evidently caused only superficial damage, because he was neither on fire nor was he smoking. What happened to the third 109, I do not know.

"I reformed the squadron which had given chase to the other enemy aircraft and since Marmite and Sweepstakes were still calling bandits in the same area, we ran a short patrol, but it proved uneventful."

Right: While encounters were infrequent, Thunderbolts did intercept V-1 "buzz bombs," as they operated within the same altitudes.

Left: The distinctive and striking red-checkered cowling identifies this airplane as a 492nd Fighter Squadron Thunderbolt.

Lt. Albert Boyette, flying as the number-three man in Maj. Orwat's second flight, scored the only confirmed kill of the day: "I got on the tail of a 109 and quickly had it smoking, going down in black-gray smoke which turned to a complete white. Checking back to clear my tail, I noticed one on [wingman] Lt. Hovde's tail and pulled around to get him. The Jerry started to leave of his own accord, so I started up to help Maj. Orwat who was in a Lufberry with three enemy planes. I started turning with another 109 to get a shot at him. The Jerry broke the turn and I closed to 75yd [69m], pouring on the bullets. He was streaming white smoke and was in a diving turn about 1,000ft [305m] above a hill. I then ran into some flak and pulled up to get back into the fight."

Enemy fighters were not the only threat the P-47s tackled. The V-1 flying-bomb menace had begun in June 1944 when the first of Hitler's "wonder weapons" was launched at London on the 13th. By the

aircraft over the Channel: "I was leading Sherwood Red Flight back from a glide-bombing mission. About mid-Channel, I was at 7,500ft [2,286m] and I noticed a white light just above the overcast at about two o'clock to me at 3,000ft [914m]. I thought it was a jet-propelled aircraft and immediately went after it. I closed in dead astern and fired, observing strikes all over the ship. These first strikes didn't seem to be vital, for the aircraft continued on its way. It was not until I made another similar attack that the aircraft burst into flames and went straight down, exploding when it hit the water. There was a big explosion, which shot a geyser of water up to about 400 or 500ft [122 or 152m]."

Left: *The 20mm Flakvierling 38 was the standard German light antiaircraft gun in 1944–45.*

As the 9th Air Force P-47 groups moved to the continent, the "doodlebug" encounters tapered off somewhat. However, when Lt. Tom DeGraffenreid was in the air, testing a newly received P-47 west of Ashford, Kent, he sighted an inbound V-1. He turned to attack it, but before he could do so, an RAF Spitfire opened fire and "the bug exploded in the air." He then spied another bug on about the same course at about 1,300ft [396m]. He dove down and turned into it to make the attack and came up under it, dead astern. His airspeed at this time was 360mph [579kmh] and he appeared to be gaining on the bug. He fired one burst of about 30 rounds and then another of about three–four seconds and the bug rolled over to the left and went down, exploding on impact. As the Allies advanced across Europe, the P-47 vs. V-1 encounters became fewer and farther between, with the majority of the V-1s being intercepted by RAF home defense Spitfires.

campaign's peak in the fall of 1944, more than a hundred of the gyroscopically guided bombs were being launched toward England every day. A sophisticated network of early-warning systems, fighter defenses, and antiaircraft guns was quickly established in response and proved effective in reducing the threat.

While aerial gunfire was the most effective method of bringing down a V-1, pilots were instructed to use extreme caution, since the accidental detonation of the Buzz Bomb's warhead would bring down both missile and interceptor. A week after the first V-1s began hitting England, 1st Lt. David Johnston of the 365th Fighter Squadron encountered an unknown

Left: *Pilots of the 492nd Fighter Squadron. In front is Capt. Bill DiStefano, who scored three air-to-air kills against the Japanese on his first combat tour in the CBI Theater.*

On Leave in the ETO

"Before long, everyone will have had the opportunity to visit one or more of the famous European cities. The facilities afforded both enlisted men and officers while on leave are many and luxurious. Although the initial cost is small, the overall expenditure is great, but no one cares about that. After all, it's the opportunity to relax and enjoy oneself—money is no object, but more of it would certainly come in handy."

—86th Fighter Group Monthly History, 1945

A three-day pass to Paris could do wonders for morale. Once the city was liberated in August 1944, it became a hotspot for off-duty GIs trying escape the rigors of combat. Like Paris, most European cities liberated by US forces were an instant draw when soldiers and airmen were given a reprieve from the frontlines or from flying combat missions. Naples, Pisa, Brussels, Liege, and Marseilles all were mysterious new destinations for GIs who had more than likely never left their hometown before joining the service.

Left: *Italy, at least those parts not engulfed in war, was a dream destination for leave. Here we see Lt. James Thomas of the 346th Fighter Squadron on pass, walking along the Pisa waterfront.*

took for granted when he was back in the States. Things like a soft bed and clean sheets, real honest-to-god plumbing facilities, and hot and cold running maids, coca colas and ice cream sodas, beer and Glen Miller's band, subways and bright lights, high heels and opera-length nylons. Paree had all of these and lots more. The Louvre, the Eiffel Tower, the Arc de Triomphe, Notre Dame, and a hundred others. As everyone knows, these are 'must' places on the tourist's docket, but a GI's fancy especially one outta the Black Forest runs more to bright lights and

As the war continued on, leave and furloughs became more frequent. By February 1945, the 373rd Fighter Group's 411th Fighter Squadron had been able to rotate the majority of its officers and enlisted men through the furlough schedule. The 86th Fighter Group spent most of its time in Italy, first flying A-36 Apache dive-bombers before transitioning to the Thunderbolt in the summer of 1944. By war's end, the group was flying as part of the XII TAC attached to the 9th Air Force in Germany, and those members who were able to take leave availed themselves of the sights and sounds of Paris. The group monthly history for May 1945 continued: "It is really remarkable how one forgets about 'civilization' and all the little things he just sorta

Right: *The Army printed Pocket Guides for every region its forces entered.*

POCKET GUIDE TO THE CITIES OF BELGIUM AND LUXEMBOURG

POCKET GUIDE TO THE CITIES OF SOUTHERN FRANCE

laughter like those offered at the Trocadero or the Moulin Rouge, even at the rapid pocket-emptying price of 60–70 Francs per shot of cognac!"

But not everyone was able to take a three-day pass or a two-week furlough, and mission tempo often only allowed twenty-four hours off before getting back into the cockpit to do it all over again. Most units felt it was mandatory to use whatever resources were available to create officers' and enlisted men's clubs, or at least a group club. When the 48th Fighter Group moved into their new accommodations, a former German military school, setting up the club was among the first priorities: "A fine new officer's club was conceived and furnished in the military academy. Lt. Lamb built an elegant bar and Lt. Wood painted ten thousand dollars' worth of murals on the walls. The first party was held on October 23 with nurses in attendance. Much of the work went to naught, however, when Ninth Army ousted us and plans were made for a group club."

Hand in hand with the relaxation facilities came the showers. Deprived of hot running water for sometimes months on end, GIs used all available assets to cobble together the comforts of home, including showers with adequate water pressure and hot and cold water. For the 48th Fighter Group, "A very elaborate shower was set up in what was once a German latrine building. A small motor was fixed with a switch so that the shower operated with an almost civilian atmosphere. Two belly tanks, one with hot water and one with cold water, were employed so that the ablutionist could regulate the temperature of the water to his satisfaction. The power for the shower was obtained from a battery cart while the actual shower motor was a fuel pump from a P-47."

Below: Members of the 78th Fighter Group and 79th Service Group stand engrossed as they watch the Bing Crosby USO Show at 8th Air Force Station F-357, Duxford, England on September 2, 1944.

410th Fighter Squadron's Big Day

In the spring of 1945, the war was rapidly drawing to its conclusion, but German resistance had intensified significantly as the Allies entered Germany. Armed reconnaissance missions were flown frequently to locate, identify, and destroy enemy forces before they could pose a significant problem for troops on the ground. 1st Lt. Talmadge Ambrose was leading his flight on one such mission on April 8, 1945, when a formation of Focke-Wulfs was sighted.

"While on an armed recce in the Hanover area, twenty–thirty Fw 190s were called in. I led the squadron on this occasion, so I ordered all bombs jettisoned and led my flight in attack, directing the remaining flights to cover us. The 190s were coming in a string out of the sun and our flight attacked the middle of the hostile group. Following the enemy aircraft to the deck, I chose one 190 and closing to 50yd [46m], gave him a short burst with strikes noted from nose to tail. I then put another burst into the cockpit and as the enemy pilot jettisoned his canopy in preparation for parachuting, I gave him another burst. He then abandoned his aircraft and I saw his parachute open, although I turned off before I saw his plane crash.

"I was now at 5,000ft [1,524m] and after dispatching the first 190, I turned into four more. They immediately split and, choosing one of the 190s, I got on his tail and fired, registering strikes all over the ship. The plane emitted smoke and fire and, going out of control, plunged earthward. Going to the aid of Red 2, I didn't actually see the plane crash, nor did I see the pilot bail out. However, Lt. D.D.A. Duncan, flying Red 3 position, saw the plane continue to weave crazily and eventually explode upon crashing.

"At this time, four more 190s jumped me and I was able to maneuver my P-47 in such a manner as to put one 190 before me before we went into a Lufberry. Somehow, I lost the three 190s on my tail and, getting in close to the fourth enemy aircraft, gave him two bursts. The second

> *3*
>
> We've really been giving the Krauts hell lately. You oughta see what one of these bombs does to a building. One second there's a building—poof—next second, no building. Our main targets, however, are trains, tanks, trucks or any kind of vehicular traffic. After we dive bomb we go back and strafe. These fifty-calibers don't do much to a tank (takes a bomb to get one of them) but they sure play hell with trucks and trains. We don't do much strafing on the deck—the flak is too damned intense. Once in

burst centered in and about the cockpit and evidently it killed the pilot for, spinning and weaving, the 190 spun in from approximately 1,000ft [305m].

"Once more I was attacked by four 190s and for approximately four minutes, I tried every trick and maneuver I knew to shake them off. In the meanwhile, I tried to straighten out and set course, but still they remained with me, obliging me to turn,

Left: One of Irwin Hollowell's many letters to his brother explaining that machine-gun fire wouldn't take out an enemy tank, "it takes a bomb to get one of them."

Below: A 373rd Thunderbolt sits patiently awaiting its next mission at Le Culot, Belgium, during the last months of the war.

split-S, break, and dive. However, after the four minutes had elapsed, three of the four 190s turned and headed east. The fourth remained on my tail and I immediately began a Lufberry to the right. Evidently this enemy pilot was inexperienced for after two turns, I got on his tail and put a burst into his fuselage. Instantly, he did a half-snap roll and went straight in, exploding violently as he crashed. I descended to take pictures then climbed to 10,000ft [3,048m] and returned to base alone."

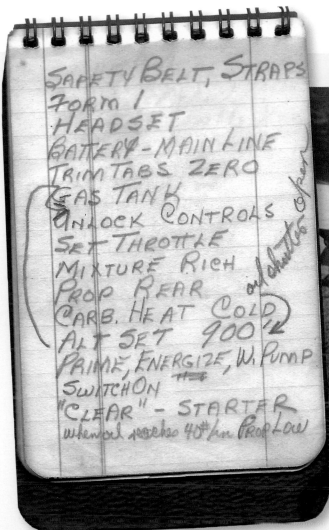

Left: Revealing the priorities of a P-47 combat pilot in-theater, here we see Lt. Irwin Hollowell's kneeboard with his hand-written before-takeoff checklist.

Above: The M41 20lb (9kg) fragmentation bomb was ideal against soft-skinned vehicles and troops. They were usually mounted in clusters of six around a central rack.

Ambrose's second element leader, 2nd Lt. Daniel D.A. Duncan had an equally successful day, shooting down another four Focke-Wulfs: "At 1520hrs on April 8, 1945, this squadron attacked a formation of twenty–thirty Fw 190s over the Hildensheim airfield. I was flying Red 3 position and the enemy aircraft approached at 13,000ft [3,962m] in a 12 o'clock high position, gradually letting down in a left turn, thus putting them on our right. The squadron leader gave the order to attack and we immediately closed on the 190s. In the resultant melee, I saw a 190 close on my leader's tail and I immediately closed on the Fw's tail approaching to 60yd [55m]. I fired a four-second burst and before I could observe the strikes, the enemy aircraft rolled over, spun crazily trailing white smoke, and I saw him crash below. Evidently the pilot had been killed, for no chute was seen to open and as the 190 descended, it had no semblance of control.

"Meanwhile, I noticed that there was another 190 who had closed on my tail and when I observed he was but approximately 30yd [27m] behind, I split-S'd. Lt. I. T. Hollowell, flying Red 4, then fired upon this 190 and after Red 4 broke off from the attack, I saw the pilot of the 190 bail out while his plane crashed. Glancing below in the direction of the airfield, I saw Red 1 and Red 2 in combat with approximately eight 190s. I chose a 190 that was close to Red 2's tail and when I had approached to within 40yd [37m] and was about to fire, the enemy pilot jettisoned his canopy and parachuted to earth while his aircraft crashed. I then chandelled up to gain altitude and when I observed three 190s chasing Red Leader, I dove and fired on one 190 with 90 degrees deflection, scoring hits on the wings and fuselage. This 190 then leveled out and headed east. I turned back to aid Red Leader and this time, he had four hostile aircraft on his tail. I pulled up behind one of the 190s and the enemy craft pulled into a straight climb and I tried to pull up underneath him. Before I had the chance, the pilot then jettisoned his canopy and bailed out. However, his chute split wide open and he fell to earth, while his aircraft augered in below. I then returned to chase another 190 from Red 2's tail and fired at the 190 using 60-degree deflection. However, knowing that I would overshoot my target, I chandelled up and when I looked again, he was lost from view. I then joined Red 2 and Yellow 4 and returned to base."

Island Hopping

"I was alone. Every pilot was alone. I kept diving, strafing, pulling up, and climbing to dive again. I made passes from stern to bow and from ahead. . . . The big baby many not have been a battleship, but it was long enough and wide enough and had enough firepower for a battleship! Passing over it was like passing too close over a blast furnace."

—Col. Gwen Atkinson, Commanding Officer, 58th Fighter Group, December 26, 1944

By comparison to the European Theater, the number of P-47s deployed to the Pacific was rather small. Only four fighter groups and two additional squadrons used the P-47D in combat, with the two squadrons only operating the type for a few weeks before transitioning to the P-38. The early Thunderbolts were not conducive to operations in the South Pacific, where the immense over-water distances from base to target would be impossible for the range-limited P-47.

The first Thunderbolt unit assigned to the 5th Air Force was Col. Neel Kearby's 348th Fighter Group. Arriving in 1943, the group flew its first combat missions from Port Moresby in mid-summer. The majority of these missions were escorting bombers to the Japanese bases on New Guinea's northern shore at Lae and Salamaua. The 348th proved that the P-47 could be an effective weapon in the Pacific and despite the better maneuverability of Japanese fighters, they didn't stand a chance against the Thunderbolt's devastating eight .50-caliber machine guns.

By late in 1943, the veteran 35th Fighter Group turned in their P-38s in favor of Thunderbolts. The 35th had been one of the first fighter groups to enter combat in the Pacific and had flown P-39s (and the export variant P-400) and P-38s since May 1942. With the capture of

Left: P-47D-2-RE 42-8139 from Col. Neel Kearby's 348th Fighter Group over New Guinea in mid-1943. The 348th was the first group to take the Thunderbolt into combat in the Pacific.

Salamaua and Lae in September 1943, the 35th and 348th moved to New Guinea's northern coast and took over Nadzab and Finschafen airfields respectively.

The third group to arrive in the Southwest Pacific was the 58th Fighter Group, which had been organized as a training unit in the United States before being earmarked for overseas deployment. The group arrived in Australia in late 1943 and began conducting combat operations from Dobodura, New Guinea, by the beginning of 1944. The 58th specialized in ground attack and provided close support for Allied forces, advancing as the island nation was liberated slowly but surely. By November 1944, the 58th moved yet again, this time several hundred miles north and west to participate in the campaign to retake the Philippines.

While the 348th, 35th, and 58th Fighter Groups made up the bulk of the P-47 presence in the Pacific Theater from 1943 through the end of 1944, the 318th Fighter Group was the sole Central Pacific Theater Thunderbolt group, having first provided air defense for the Hawaiian Islands and later entered combat in support of operations to capture Saipan in the Marianas chain in June 1944. The 318th, like the 58th, operated in close coordination with US Marines on Saipan. The 318th's performance during the latter half of 1944 was a major factor in the group being chosen as the first fighter group to convert to the new P-47N in the spring of 1945.

Medal of Honor

Col. Neel Kearby's 348th Fighter Group introduced the P-47 to the Pacific in the summer of 1943, and quickly proved that, despite its detractors, the Thunderbolt could be an effective fighter for the theater. Kearby scored his first pair of kills on September 4, 1943, and followed with a third on the 15th. But on a mission over Wewak in October, Kearby achieved ace status by destroying six enemy airplanes on a single mission. "I was leading a flight of four P-47s on a fighter sweep over Wewak on October 11, 1943. We took off from Port Moresby at 0715hrs local and landed at Tsili Tsili at 0830hrs to refuel. We took off from Tsili Tsili at 0915hrs and arrived over Wewak at 1030hrs local time at 23,000ft [7,010m]. The weather was excellent with a few scattered clouds between 2,000 and 8,000ft [610 and 2,438m]. We saw a number of aircraft parked on Boram strip and one aircraft taxiing on the runway. He did not take off.

"The fuel in our belly tanks had been consumed, so we dropped them to increase our speed and conserve fuel. At 1115hrs, one Zeke was sighted at 9 o'clock below 20,000ft [6,096m]. I came in on him from 7 o'clock above and opened fire at 1,500ft [457m]. He took no evasive

Both left: A 5th Air Force badge. Also Col. Neel Kearby, CO of the 348th Fighter Group, awarded the Medal of Honor for actions on October 11, 1943.

action, caught fire, and dived into the sea. We climbed back up to 26,000ft [7,925m] and at about 1125hrs saw about thirty-six fighters: Tonys, Haps, and Zekes and twelve bombers, of an unidentified type approaching from the southeast along the coast.

"The fighters were at about 10,000 to 15,000ft [3,048m to 4,572m] and the bombers at about 5,000ft [1,524m]. We came in from above. I opened fire on a Zeke at 1,500ft [457m] and closed as he burst into flames. No evasive action was taken. I turned slightly and opened fire at 1,500ft [457m] from 7 o'clock on a Hap which burst into flames, taking no evasive action. I looked up and another Hap was turning slightly to the left. I closed to 1,500ft [457m] and opened fire from slightly above and from about 8 o'clock. He burst into flames after he had passed beyond my sights in the turn. I was indicating over 400mph [644kmh] during this period.

By this time the Nips realized we were there, so I pulled up sharply to about 20,000ft [6,096m] and saw Capt. Dunham. I joined him and we started home. Immediately at 2 o'clock below at about 10,000ft [3,048m], I saw Capt. Moore in a P-47 with one Tony about 3,000ft [914m] to the rear and another Tony about 3,000ft [914m] behind the first one. Capt. Moore was headed for home. I turned and came in at 400mph [644kmh] on the tail of the rear Tony, opening fire at 1,500ft [457m]. He took no evasive action and burst into flames.

"I closed for the other which was on Capt. Moore's tail, but he must have seen me as he turned and dove down in front of me. I opened fire from about 2,000ft [610m], closing in, and saw tracers going into him and pieces of his wing and fuselage flying off. I did not see him catch fire, nor did I see him crash, as I did not have time to watch him.

"Capt. Moore saw this Tony burst into flames and crash in the sea. He then turned back toward Wewak and I turned with him. Tonys were all over the sky. I made another pass at a Tony from about 10 o'clock but [the] deflection was wrong. I looked behind and saw a Tony closing on my tail, so I dived for the nearby clouds. We were now at about 7,000ft

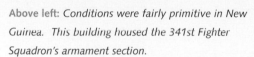

Above left: *Conditions were fairly primitive in New Guinea. This building housed the 341st Fighter Squadron's armament section.*

Above right: *P-47D-21-RE was the third airplane assigned to Lt. Col. Robert Rowland and the third to carry the "Miss Mutt/Pride of Lodi Ohio" artwork.*

Right: *Card sent to Sgt. Francis Malcolm, an armorer with the 341st Fighter Squadron, 348th Fighter Group, from his girlfriend.*

[2,134m]. When coming out of the clouds, I could no longer see the Tony. I climbed to 15,000ft [4,572m] and called the flight. They all checked in and we proceeded to Lae and landed there at 1240hrs.

"Capt. Moore destroyed two fighters and Capt. Dunham one. Maj. Gallagher had chased a Zeke into the clouds and was unable to find another enemy aircraft when he came out. We refueled at Lae and returned to Port Moresby."

Kearby went on to score thirteen additional kills after his Medal of Honor mission, bringing his total to twenty-two confirmed. On March 5, 1944, however, Kearby, Maj. Sam Blair, and Capt. Bill Dunham were again over Wewak looking for Japanese airplanes when they attacked a formation of fifteen Ki-43 Oscars. Kearby's first pass destroyed one, but three of the Oscars managed to get on his tail. Kearby's wingmen were able to destroy two, but the third's guns found their mark and Kearby's Thunderbolt, "Fiery Ginger IV," went straight into the jungle.

Col. Neel Kearby's Medal of Honor Citation

Near Wewak, New Guinea, October 11, 1943. For conspicuous gallantry and intrepidity above and beyond the call of duty in action with the enemy, Col. Kearby volunteered to lead a flight of four fighters to reconnoiter the strongly defended enemy base at Wewak. Having observed enemy installations and reinforcements at four airfields, and secured important tactical information, he saw an enemy fighter below him, made a diving attack and shot it down in flames. The small formation then sighted approximately twelve enemy bombers accompanied by thirty-six fighters. Although his mission had been completed, his fuel was running low, and the numerical odds were twelve to one, he gave the signal to attack. Diving into the midst of the enemy airplanes he shot down three in quick succession. Observing one of his comrades with two enemy fighters in pursuit, he destroyed both enemy aircraft. The enemy broke off in large numbers to make a multiple attack on his airplane but despite his peril he made one more pass before seeking cloud protection. Coming into the clear, he called his flight together and led them to a friendly base. Col. Kearby brought down six enemy aircraft in this action, undertaken with superb daring after his mission was completed.

Battle Over Pagan Island

With the capture of Saipan and Tinian in the summer of 1944, American B-29 long-range bombers now had bases within striking distance of the Japanese home islands. Japanese forces remaining in the area around the Mariana Islands were based on several rocky outcrops, including Pagan Island, 200 miles [322km] to the north. Airstrikes on Saipan originating from Pagan, Truk, and Iwo Jima were more a nuisance than strategically significant, but the 318th Fighter Group, already providing air defense cover for the islands, was now tasked with locating and destroying the Japanese raiders on their home fields.

Maj. Warren Roesser of the 333rd Fighter Squadron led the squadron's first sweep over Pagan and scored his second kill on November 3. "On Friday, November 3, 1944, at 0445hrs, I was airborne with twelve other P-47s for a strike on Pagan Island, carrying only a full load of .50-cal ammo. We arrived over the target at 0545hrs at which time I left the

Above: *"Spitten Kitten" of the 73rd Fighter Squadron prepares to launch from the deck of the USS Manila Bay on June 23 in order to intercept a flight of Japanese D3A "Val" dive-bombers.*

formation to go below the clouds and find a special target assigned me by Group S-2. Just as I broke through the cloud layer, I spotted a twin-engine airplane approaching the runway from the southwest at 500ft [152m], about ½ mile [0.8km] off shore. It was painted olive drab and had large red roundels on the fuselage and wing. Its wingtips were square.

"I immediately attacked in a 60-degree dive and caught him just as he was about to land. He evidently saw me, for I just had time to rip an extremely short bust (½ second) into him at less than 300ft [91m], when he veered off to the right of the runway and crashed up against a bomb shelter.

"My first burst seemed to enter his port engine. After he crashed, I made three more runs, firing approximately three–four-second bursts on each one. On the second run, the plane exploded and burned, setting off ammo in the bomber and apparently firing his bombs or fuel tanks. No one was seen to leave the plane. At a second glance, the plane looked very much like a [P1Y2] Francis."

Lt. Robert Stone witnessed Roesser's kill and was able to confirm its destruction. "We were breaking away from the target. I was in a vertical bank, going about 400mph [644kmh] coming off the target. Off to the right, approximately 200yd [183m] was a Jap plane putting his wheels down on the final approach to the runway. I immediately called him in to my flight leader, but due to radio interferences, he was unable to hear me. A few seconds later, Maj. Roesser sighted the same plane and attacked it. He started the left engine on fire and the plane crashed into a bomb shelter. Maj. Roesser made three strafing passes on the plane and on the second, the plane exploded and caught fire. I would identify the plane as a Francis or [J1N1] Irving. It was definitely destroyed. It was silver colored and I did not observe any distinctive markings other than the large red balls on the fuselage." Additional strikes against Pagan were flown throughout the month, but no enemy aircraft were encountered in the air until November 27.

Lt. William Fancher led a flight of four Thunderbolts on a fighter sweep over Pagan, scoring his first and only kill of the war: "I was approximately 3 miles [5km] southeast of the peninsula on the east shore of Pagan when I sighted one Zeke about 2 miles [3km] northwest of Bandeera Headland. He was heading south at 1,000ft [305m]. The Zeke made a turn toward the runway as I fired a one-second burst head-on at 300yd [274m]. He returned fire. After we passed, the Zeke made a sharp left turn and I made a tight climbing turn to the right. As the Zeke leveled out, I was pulling onto his tail at 1,000yd [914m]. I opened fire and closed to 100ft [30m]. At 300ft [91m], the Zeke started to slowly drop his right wing. As I closed, he rolled almost on his back and hit the water in the lake near the northwest shore of the island.

Left: *After the 318th's support of Marines on Saipan, the group was awarded a unit commendation.*
Far left: *Uniform of SSgt. Leon Stehman of Johnstown, PA, who served as a crew chief on 19th Fighter Squadron P-47s and P-38s*

me because I got in a good burst before he turned off to the northwest. "I observed many hits in the Zeke's wing roots before he disappeared under my right wing. Immediately after this, my wingman Lt. Williams (Violet 26-2) called me on the radio saying that the Zeke had crashed on the north taxiway. My flight then pulled up to 2,000ft [610m] west of the island to observe the crashed airplane. We noticed that it was not burning, so we strafed it in string formation. It then burst into flames."

Lt. Durwood Williams, flying DeYonker's wing witnessed the action: "As we approached Pagan, we spotted a Zeke at about 100ft [30m] over Bandeera Headland. I followed Lt. Deyonker as he made a head-on attack against the Zeke. The Zeke passed under Lt. Deyonker and flew straight for about 100yd [91m]. It then lost altitude rapidly and crashed on the north taxiway."

Below: *The 318th's first assignment after receiving P-47s was the air defense of Hawaii. P-47D-11-RE 42-75304 of the 333rd Fighter Squadron is seen here flying over the beaches on Oahu.*

"Before the Zeke crashed, I observed several hits in his wings and on the canopy. Very slight turns in both directions were the only evidences of evasive action. The pilot did not bail out."

Lt. James DeYonker, leading another flight from the 333rd, also sighted a Zeke and moved in for the kill: "As we were approaching Pagan from the southwest, I spotted one Zeke over Bandeera Headland at 100ft [30m] altitude, headed east. I immediately attacked, making a head-on pass. The pilot of the Zeke evidently did not see

Anti-Ship Fighter-Bombers

The 58th Fighter Group arrived in the Southwest Pacific in late 1943 and began flying combat operations by early February 1944. While initially tasked with bomber escort missions, the 58th easily transitioned to the ground-attack role as the American island-hopping campaign continued. When the 11th Airborne Division seized the first airfield on Mindoro in mid-December 1944, two squadrons of the 58th—the 69th and 311th—were among the first to arrive at Hill Field.

By the evening of December 26, word came down that a significant Japanese naval force consisting of two cruisers and six destroyers was headed for Hill Field to bombard it and possibly attempt to recapture the airfield. Col. Gwen Atkinson, commanding officer of the 58th Fighter Group, volunteered his two squadrons, and as darkness fell they readied for action.

"We had just thirty-two planes—our chunky, sweet P-47s—available. There were between sixty and seventy pilots ready to go. I called squadron and flight commanders together and asked for the names of the thirty-one most experienced pilots. I intended to, and did fly, the 32nd plane.

"Shortly word came from the airstrip that all bombs were many miles away, on the west coast of Mindoro. We had just moved up there three days before and there had not yet been time to get all of our supplies in. If we waited for the bombs to be brought to us, the task force would be in before we could hit it. I informed HQ of the situation and thought someone had gone mad when I was told to attack the task force with or without bombs.

"The thirty-one chosen pilots were called together and given the picture, or as much of it as I knew. It had been reported then that there was a battleship and a heavy cruiser in the task force and there was some air support. Making strafing passes on anything larger than a destroyer is damn risky at any time. At night, when you cannot see to keep protective formation, it's a one-way ticket.

"Arriving at the strip I found that there was a red alert. Nip planes were heading for us. We hurriedly got in our planes, taxied out, and took off. As soon as six of us had rendezvoused, we headed up the coast to the given position of the convoy. The last few had to take off between attacks by the Nips and between two of our planes that had cracked up on the soft runway and were burning.

"After a brief search, we found the task force 15 miles [24km] up the coast and 5 miles [8km] offshore. The ships were dark blobs on the water

Right: Operating from rough Pacific landing grounds necessitated a vigilant maintenance program in order to keep the P-47 airworthy. Dirt and grit easily clogged filters, fouled intakes, and made operating combat aircraft far more difficult.

marked by phosphorescent wakes. I knew we could do no formation fighting in the darkness. Our best chance lay in each man fighting his own fight, going in on the ships from all angles. There was grave danger of our ramming into each other, so I ordered that all passes be made from west to east, so we could all be going in the same direction. Too, this would silhouette the ships against what light there was.

"Picking a ship, I went down for a first pass. As I opened fire, I was spotted by my tracers—there had been no time to remove them as we usually do for night fighting—and every ship opened up on me. It was as if a volcano had erupted to blast open the night.

Left: P-47D-23-RA 42-27995 from the 311th Fighter Squadron returns to base after a mission over northern Luzon in the Philippines.

"I saw none of my own planes. I was alone. Every pilot was alone. I kept diving, strafing, pulling up, and climbing to dive again. I made passes from stern to bow and from ahead. I held my fire until I could see the superstructure of a ship so that I could do all the damage possible. I strafed all of the ships, taking them one by one. The big baby may not have been a battleship, but it was long enough and wide enough and had enough firepower for a battleship! Passing over it was like passing too close over a blast furnace. After the fourth or fifth pass, I called our ground controller and told him we had just enough gas left to get to Leyte Island. We had been ordered to land on Leyte, in case the Japs managed to get ashore at Mindoro and capture our airstrip. The controller just answered 'attack the target.' So, I forgot the gas and kept strafing until my last gun put-putted out.

"Leyte was 300 miles [483km] away. I had enough gas left for about two hours of flying. After an hour and forty minutes flying on instruments, I came over the island but was a long way from safe. There was little hope of finding the airfield in that murk and I had only about thirty minutes of gas left. My savior was the ground controller at that Leyte airstrip. He was good. He took me over—his instructions flew my plane for me until suddenly I saw the flattened beam of a searchlight filtering through that soupy sky. Then like magic, a hole appeared in the murk. Through it I saw the most beautiful sight I shall ever see—the green lights that bordered the landing strip!

"Final reports on the battle showed both of the heavy ships badly damaged, two of the destroyers sunk, and a third damaged. A captured Jap navy petty officer has said that the shelling was so poor because all range-finders and automatic aiming devices for the ships' guns had been shot out."

Above: "Kisit" from the 310th Fighter Squadron undergoing basic engine maintenance.

Left: The E-6B "whiz wheel" allowed pilots to compute rates of fuel consumption, true airspeed, and wind drift.

The final intelligence assessment referenced by Col. Atkinson was incorrect, as only one Japanese destroyer was sunk; it was finished off by US PT boats operating in the area. Yet the majority of the damage inflicted was from .50-caliber ammunition from two P-47 and one P-40 squadron, damaging or destroying so significant a portion of the Japanese fire-control systems that they were unable to deliver an effective bombardment of Hill Field and were forced to withdraw. The 58th Fighter Group was awarded the Distinguished Unit Citation for their participation in the battle, and Col. Atkinson was awarded the Distinguished Service Cross for his intrepid and selfless leadership during the engagement.

R&R in the Pacific and CBI Theaters

"If you have just arrived in India, or if you have been up country and have come down here for a brief respite, you are equally in need of a little rest and relaxation. You want to have as much fun as possible while you're here? Surprise: that is exactly what the Army wants for you, too."

—*Calcutta Key*

The Pacific and CBI proved more difficult than Europe for the fortunate GI looking to get away from the horrors of combat for a little while. The first major obstacle was the sheer distance between where his unit was based and any form of civilization.

The Southwest Pacific nevertheless offered a multitude of options. For the ambitious, Hawaii was a welcome destination that had a fairly large population of American women either in uniform or working for the military at Pearl Harbor, Schofield Barracks, or one of the smaller posts. Travel to and from Hawaii, however, was time consuming and uncertain. Many chose to head south, rather than east, and Australia welcomed the American GI with open arms.

Melbourne, Brisbane, and Sydney were all prime destinations for GIs on leave and were fairly close to feeling like home for many of them. Numerous clubs for American servicemen popped up across eastern Australia, many of which were run by the American Red Cross. A GI on leave just needed to make contact with the Red Cross upon his arrival in Australia and they would be able to direct him to the best living accommodations, places to visit, and other attractions.

Clubs like the "Dug Out" in Melbourne also catered to GIs on furlough, providing the "best dances in Melbourne" on a near-nightly basis. The "American Centre" in Brisbane also gave a little taste of home, giving GIs on leave from New Guinea a place where they could relax in comfort, enjoy game rooms and bowling alleys, and partake of the readily available hamburgers and coffee at will. Yet apart from the city attractions, the South Pacific was a veritable paradise when the Japanese weren't shooting at you. GIs arriving in Australia often chose to spend their leave relaxing on the beach, fishing, or partaking in any number of fun activities on Australia's coastline.

Things were somewhat closer and easier to reach in the CBI, where the Indian cities of Karachi, Madras, and Calcutta all had relatively modern accommodations for 10th Air Force personnel. Travel in exotic India was popular, especially to sights like the famed Taj Mahal. GIs on leave could expect to stay in a hotel with clean sheets and running water and, in spite of the continuing oppressive heat and humidity, have a comfortable stay.

The US Army had a significant presence in Calcutta. A serviceman's guide to the city, its people, attractions, and sights called the *Calcutta Key*, was issued to soldiers arriving on leave. One passage ran as follows: "If you have just arrived in India, or if you have been up country and have come down here for a brief respite, you are equally in need of a little rest and relaxation. You want to have as much fun as possible while you're here? Surprise: that is exactly what the Army wants for you, too. Unfortunately, in comparison with American standards, there is a limited amount of recreational facilities in Calcutta; but everything that is here is yours. Enjoy it but don't abuse it. You have a date with Calcutta; treat her like a lady and you will find her to be one."

Leave in Calcutta or Brisbane was a short-term respite from the rigors of combat. However, temporary reassignment for rest and recuperation (R&R) allowed GIs to return to the United States for thirty days. Unlike a furlough or in-theater leave, the GI was still on duty and did have reporting responsibilities to his higher headquarters. Yet he would be able to see friends and family, travel, and put the war temporarily out of his mind.

As the war drew to a close, the thirty-day R&R was increased to forty-five days with the anticipation of the cessation of hostilities. *CBI Roundup*, the theater newspaper, ran the following on March 29, 1945, regarding the updated R&R policy: "The 30 days previously granted India-Burma Theater personnel on temporary duty for a recuperation period in the United States has been extended to 45 days, it was announced this week by Lt. Gen. Dan I. Sultan, Theater Commander. Personnel eligible for this temporary duty were individuals who were selected through their respective commanding officers. They are key men whom the unit commander classifies as occupying positions requiring skills difficult to replace. Personnel become eligible to apply for temporary duty in the States upon completion of 24 months unbroken service abroad. Upon completion of their temporary duty in the U.S., they will return to their duties here in this Theater. The amended order went into effect Mar. 14 and applies to men now in or en route to the States for recuperation, with the exception of those unfortunates already at a stateside port of embarkation or en route to one for return here."

Prayer books from a number of Army Air Force servicemen, including a book of Jewish scripture.

Cpl. Irving J. Levine
Hq. 414th Fighter Grp.

THE WHITE HOUSE
WASHINGTON

To the Members of the

ABRIDGED PRAYER BOOK FOR JEWS IN THE ARMED FORCES OF THE UNITED STATES

DEVOTIONAL MANUAL

Greater love than this no man hath

lay down his his friends

RESTING THE SOUL *Although the majority of the enlisted men's time was taken up with intense work, the occasional day off did occur. Religious services for all faiths were also conducted by the group chaplain, who was trained to minister to all.*

Formosa Firefight

With the Joint Chiefs' decision, in October 1944, to bypass Formosa in favor of the invasion of Luzon in the Philippines, an entire Japanese field army and a significant Japanese naval presence were left stranded on the island, including air forces totaling more than 1,200 aircraft. These aircraft posed a significant threat to B-29s flying from airfields in China, and against planned operations in northern Luzon and the Ryukyu Islands. A significant US Navy air campaign against Japanese forces on Formosa in October 1944 destroyed roughly one-third of those aircraft, but missions over Formosa by USAAF aircraft became a regular occurrence in early 1945. The 35th Fighter Group moved to Mangaldan airfield on the west coast of Luzon on January 27, and by the 30th the group's 39th Fighter Squadron was conducting long-range fighter sweeps over Formosa, nearly 400 miles (644km) to the north.

Lt. Leroy Grossheusch led the 39th Fighter Squadron on January 30, 1945, scoring his second and third kills: "Lt. [Eugene] Haws, the element leader of Red Flight, sighted a possible [Ki-21] Sally at about 2,000ft [610m] in the vicinity of Taichu. I told Lt. Haws to take his element down while we covered him, but the Sally disappeared into the clouds. At this time, I saw one transition plane [used to transition pilots from trainer to advanced fighter aircraft], probably an obsolete fighter, at 2,000ft [610m]. I made a pass and observed hits in the area of the cockpit. I pulled up and made another pass, shooting it down. This plane crashed into the ground and disintegrated. I then sighted another of the same type heading west and made a pass on it, shooting it down. This

Above: Aviation engineers inspect a new runway lined with Perforated Steel Planking, or PSP, which improved the surface for landings and takeoffs.

plane crashed into the trees about 3 miles [5km] northwest of the area in which the first plane crashed.

"Lt. [Idon] Hodge, leading White Flight, made a pass on two more transition planes in the same area. He overshot and the planes turned sharply to the right. Lt. [Charles] Posey, Lt. Hodge's wingman, fired a short burst at the second plane, causing him to dive straight into the ground. I then reformed my flights, and climbing up to 7,000ft [2,134m], headed north."

Upon nearing the airdrome at Shinchiku, Lt. Haws sighted four Zekes at approximately 2,000ft (610m). Lt. Hodge and Lt. Posey made a pass on these four Zekes, followed down by Lt. Haws. Lt. Hodge fired on the Zeke to the right. This Zeke burst into flames immediately and crashed into the ground 5 miles (8km) south of the airdrome. Lt. Posey fired a three-second burst into the Zeke on the left and it burst into flames and crashed into the ground approximately ½ mile (0.9km) north of Lt. Hodge's Zeke. Lt. Haws, following, fired on one of the remaining Zekes, observing hits on the canopy and cockpit area. Lt. Haws pulled up to the left and Lt. Posey observed the Zeke going down in flames and exploded just before hitting the ground. Posey later explained:

"Lt Ervine Pratt and Lt. Eli Tueche observed three Zekes at 2,000ft [610m] off to the south of the flight and dived on them. One Zeke broke away and the other two continued flying straight and level. Lt. Pratt and Lt. Tueche latched onto the tails of these two Zekes. Lt. Pratt took the Zeke on the right and Lt. Tueche the one on the left. Lt. Pratt fired a five-second burst from about 400 to 100yd [366 to 91m] and observed continuous hits in the fuselage and cockpit area. This Zeke started to roll over on its back and went into the ground and bust into one long wall of flame. Lt. Tueche, following the Zeke on the left as it went into a left bank, led it approximately 2 radii. He fired a two-second burst from about 90 degrees and observed hits in the area of the engine and cockpit. Smoke began to stream from both sides of the engine and the plane continued into a slow turn, crashing into the ground about 50ft [15m] from Lt. Pratt's, bursting into a ball of flame. Both pilots observed these planes. After pulling up, Lt. Tueche saw me firing on the Zeke which had broken away from the original three sighted. Lt. Tueche started after us and as I was running out of ammunition, Lt. Tueche closed in and I broke off. Lt. Teuche followed the Zeke for about 5 miles [8km] before catching it. He opened fire at about 500yd [457m] and closed up to 100yd [91m], firing all the time. He observed hits on the Zeke in the tail area. The Zeke started a skid and Lt. Tueche fired another burst, observing hits in the cockpit area. The Zeke went out of control and when last observed was at 500ft [152m]. He claimed this Zeke as a probable."

Above left: "Princess Margie" from the 41st Fighter Squadron has just landed after a combat mission over the Philippines, mid 1945.
Above right: The .45 Colt M1911 was the standard sidearm carried by P-47 pilots throughout World War II..
Right: A captured Japanese Navy N1K1 "George" fighter used by US forces to train combat pilots.
Below: 35th Fighter Group Thunderbolts in formation over the Philippines in early 1945.

Lt. Posey had started to join Lt. Hodge, and in the excitement of scoring his first two kills, overtook his flight leader while attempting to get back into formation. Sighting another target, however, he continued past:. "As I overran, I sighted a [Ki-61] Tony headed for the strip at Shinkichu. I immediately did a wingover and went down after the Tony at deck level. Lt. Hodge followed me down. I fired a five-second burst from dead astern at 500yd [457m] and closed to 200yd [183m] and observed hits on the wings and tail. I then broke away to avoid the antiaircraft fire and Lt. Hodge, who was following, observed the Tony to go into a violent skid and crash into the trees on the west side of the strip, approximately 1 mile [1.6km] off."

Lt. Grossheusch was promoted to captain after his double kill on the 30th and scored another three kills on February 10. He took over as squadron commander shortly thereafter, and he ended the war as the 39th Fighter Squadron's fourth leading scorer with eight kills, all but one scored in the P-47.

CBI Jugs

"I made my bombing dive at 0940hrs to the north, released at a safe altitude, and was making a climbing turn to the left when I felt a jolt at about 4,000ft [1,219m]. I believe I was hit by ground fire, although I did not see any flashes or tracers. The engine began to backfire and miss. . . . oil started to come out of the left side of the engine."

—Capt. William Hemphill, commanding officer, 6th Fighter Squadron (Commando), April 17, 1945

With the successes of American P-40 fighter-bomber units in the China-Burma-India (CBI) Theater, and the fact that the theater was the lowest priority in terms of supply needs, it was not until the late spring of 1944 that P-47s began to arrive in the region. By this time, improvements in both engine and propeller had made the Thunderbolt deadly at any altitude.

At this time, the CBI Theater was the only theater of operations where US forces did not make up the bulk of the Allied combat power. The British, headquartered in India, had the largest number of ground troops in India and Burma, while the Chinese continued their war against the Japanese within China. American ground forces were limited to a small force in Burma, but two American air forces provided air support to ground elements in both regions, the 10th Air Force in India and Burma and the 14th in China.

Both air forces had fighter units assigned, but the first P-47 units to arrive in-theater were transferred from the 12th Air Force in the Mediterranean Theater. The 33rd Fighter Group's P-40s launched from the escort carriers USS *Chenango* (CVE-28) and HMS *Archer* on November 10, 1942, in support of Operation *Torch*, the invasion of North Africa. The 81st Fighter Group, flying Bell P-39

Left: Lt. Lee Mullins taxiing his P-47D-23-RA on Asansol airfield in India (in part of the country now in Pakistan), about to take off on an armed reconnaissance mission.

Airacobras, arrived in North Africa a month later. Both units flew numerous combat missions in North Africa and supported the invasions of Sicily, Salerno, and finally Anzio, before being transferred to the CBI. The groups arrived at Karachi, India, in February and March 1944, began conversion to the Thunderbolt, and by late April were declared operationally ready. Both units were assigned to the 14th Air Force and were flying combat missions in China by May. As 1944 progressed and air support requirements changed, the 33rd Fighter Group was reassigned to the 10th Air Force in December and remained there through the end of the war.

While the two transferred units were training on the P-47, the 80th Fighter Group had stood down from combat operations and began conversion to the Thunderbolt as well. The 80th had been in-theater for a year already, flying P-40s in the close air support (CAS) and interdiction roles. The "Burma Banshees" would be the first group to support Allied units in Burma with the P-47. The fourth and final groups to receive Thunderbolts in the CBI were the newly designated 5th and 6th Fighter Squadrons of the 1st Air Commando Group. The group had flown P-51A Mustangs since early 1944 and began conversion to the Thunderbolt in late summer. All four groups played a critical role in the liberation of the CBI Theater, providing desperately needed air support in an aircraft that had become synonymous with the role.

Air Defense with the 92nd

Combat missions in the CBI Theater were some of the most dangerous, yet most overlooked, of those flown by Thunderbolt pilots. The overwhelming majority of those missions conducted were ground-attack, flying through intense automatic weapons and antiaircraft fire in order to put bombs and machine-gun fire on target to aid friendly forces on the ground. Enemy aircraft were seldom encountered and therefore most pilots never got to see a hostile airplane up close during their combat tour. Those enemy aircraft that were encountered were usually night-harassment raids by small formations of Japanese medium bombers. These raids specifically targeted fighter-bomber airfields, as the P-40s and P-47s that flew from these airfields were wreaking havoc on Japanese ground forces in the area.

noticed another string of bombs hit from east to west on the south side of the runway. I came down from 5,000ft [1,524m] to 3,000ft [914m] and then to 2,000ft [610m] in a gradual let down. At this time, I was at the east end of the field going southwest.

"I then sighted a twin-engine bomber, which I identified as hostile, below and to the right of me. I had to pass over the top of the bomber and then I made a sharp turn to the right. At this point the bomber made a sharp turn to the right as well. I then crossed over him again and then made another turn to the right. I maneuvered into position to make a 30-degree

Left: Personal insecticide powder was made available to GIs to repel lice and other nasty creatures.

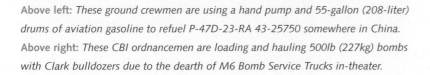

Above left: These ground crewmen are using a hand pump and 55-gallon (208-liter) drums of aviation gasoline to refuel P-47D-23-RA 43-25750 somewhere in China.
Above right: These CBI ordnancemen are loading and hauling 500lb (227kg) bombs with Clark bulldozers due to the dearth of M6 Bomb Service Trucks in-theater.

Lt. Howard A. Cox, of the 92nd Fighter Squadron, described one mission in which he took on some Japanese attackers: "I took off from Ankang at 2230hrs on August 2, 1944, on a report that Japanese bombers were approaching the field from the east. I climbed to 5,000ft [1,524m] and shortly after I reached this altitude, I saw a string of bombs hit from west to east on the runway at the field. Shortly thereafter, I

deflection shot, giving him a one-second burst. The flash of the tracers blinded me, but when I saw the plane again, I gave another one-second burst. I was at about 200yd [183m] distance on both bursts. I then noticed fires start in both engines and at the wing roots when the bomber was about 400ft [122m] from the ground. It then hit the ground and disintegrated as it hit.

"Another bomber passed over the area but no contact was made. I fired 165 rounds of .50-caliber ammunition during the attack. Since the runway had been bombed at Ankang, the ground controller radioed instructions on how to reach Hangchung. I landed at Hangchung at 0045hrs on August 3, 1944. The night landing facilities there were very

Above: A graphic representing the total impact of the 14th Air Force on the Japanese war machine from 1942 to October 1944, showing the huge losses inflicted.

Above: A 91st Fighter Squadron P-47 takes off from Kwanghan airfield armed with two 165-gal (625-liter) napalm bombs.

good. During the entire flight, I was firing without the aid of a gunsight as both of the sights in my plane were out."

Lt. Cox was officially credited with a single Ki-48 "Lilly" bomber for this mission, one of 2.5 kills scored by the 92nd Fighter Squadron in both the Mediterranean and CBI Theaters. The 81st Fighter Group ended the war with only 13.5 kills, which is misleading when one looks at the combat effectiveness of this world-class fighter-bomber group.

Dual-Theater Fighter Groups — the 33rd and 81st Fighter Groups

At the end of 1943, the USAAF combat air forces in the European and Mediterranean Theaters underwent a significant reorganization. The 9th Air Force shifted its headquarters from North Africa to England, where it stood up as the tactical counterpart to the strategic 8th Air Force. The 12th Air Force then did similarly with the 15th Air Force in the Mediterranean. Those fighter groups in the MTO that had previously fallen under the 9th, like the 57th and 324th Groups, were then reassigned to the 12th, while the two American Spitfire groups assigned to the 12th were retasked to the 15th and scheduled to receive P-51s for the escort role. The majority of those fighter groups moved during the reorganization remained in the Mediterranean Theater. However, since Theater requirements were met and additional fighters were needed in China to provide escorts and air defense for the planned B-29 bases there, the 33rd and 81st Fighter Groups were reassigned to the CBI Theater at the beginning of 1944. While the units were identified for reassignment, 12th Air Force would not relinquish control until the situation around the Anzio beachhead stabilized. The Allied landings there on January 22 had initially met with minimal resistance, but the beachhead quickly bogged down into a tenuous foothold on the western Italian coast. Once the beachhead was reinforced, HQ 12th Air Force released the two groups for transfer. By March, the 14th Air Force had stood up the 312th Fighter Wing in preparation for the 33rd and 81st's arrival. The two groups turned in their P-40s and P-39s respectively upon arrival at Karachi, India, to begin conversion to the Thunderbolt. P-47s began to arrive via US Navy escort carrier at the end of March and with one hundred airplanes on hand by the 30th, both groups began transitioning to the new fighter.

Below: Most CBI-issued P-47Ds were late-model Razorbacks of the D-22-RE or D-23-RA production blocks, equipped with broad-chord propellers.

Thunderbolts Against the Odds

The Japanese-controlled town of Bhamo was the last obstacle between Allied (US, Chinese, and British) troops in Burma and Chinese troops in Yunnan, China. The Japanese had built up significant fortifications around the town, forcing the allies to lay siege for nearly a month in November–December 1944. By December 14, the airfields at Bhamo were in Allied hands, yet well within range of Japanese sniper and mortar fire. On that day, Lt. Samuel Hammer and Lt. Stedman Howarth of the 90th Fighter Squadron were patrolling the area south of Bhamo at 10,000ft [3,048m] when they spotted a friendly C-47 under attack. Leading the flight of two, Lt. Hammer quickly dove to the transport's aid. "When I first saw the enemy fighters, they were apparently strafing the parachutes which had just been dropped by a C-47. I dove sharply to the attack and by the time I had reached the point of attack, the [Ki-44] Tojos were actively attacking the C-47. The lead Tojo of four was firing into the C-47 and I could see smoke coming from the C-47. I started firing on the lead Tojo, at first observing my tracers to be passing under the enemy. The gunsight would not cooperate because of a faulty connection. When I commenced firing, the lead Tojo pulled up sharply, climbing to 1,000ft [305m], heading north. I followed closely, firing all the time. At the end of the climb, the Tojo flipped over, dived to the ground and crashed. The crash of this plane was confirmed by observation of the pilot of the C-47.

"The two Tojos of the second element had followed this and by the time of the crash of the first Tojo, they were on my tail. I commenced evasive action, pulling up sharply in a vertical reverse. The enemy attempted to follow this maneuver, but collided in mid-air when about 1,000ft [305m] above the ground. The planes fell to the ground, separating about 200 yards apart in the fall.

"Four Tojos then jumped me from above, at 1,000ft [305m] and I headed north along the road to Bhamo in level flight, indicating 310mph [499kmh] and pulling 65in [165cm] [manifold pressure]. The Tojos were able to close to 200yd [183m] in spite of my efforts to outdistance them and they continued to gain until I was clear of the mountains and

Right: This American flag was carefully hand painted on leather and then sewn onto an A-2 flight jacket.

Left: Lt. Wharton Moller of the 89th Fighter Squadron sits in his airplane on the hot runway, "bombed up" and ready to start his engine for his next dive-bombing mission over Japanese-held territory.

Above: White cowl rings identify these Thunderbolts as 88th Fighter Squadron P-47s, more than likely at Tingkawk Sakan airfield, India.

I followed it down to 700ft [213m] above the ground. It was still diving on its back at slightly more than vertical, making no attempt to recover from the dive. I do not believe it would be possible for the plane to recover from a dive at this speed at this altitude and it is my opinion that the initial attack killed the pilot. Subsequent observation of the point to which this plane was diving disclosed a large fire.

"I could not follow this plane to observe its crash because of an attack by two other Tojos. I turned toward them and they broke away, avoiding my head-on attack. After these planes had broken away, I climbed to regain altitude, attacking two single Tojos during my climb but only getting snap shots at them. I was not able to observe any bullet strikes. I climbed to 17,000ft [5,181m] in an attempt to rejoin Lt. Hammer, but I was unable to locate him. I then flew over Bhamo II landing ground and when assured by gestures that Lt. Hammer was unhurt, returned to base, landing first at Myitkyina because of gasoline shortage.

"The enemy pilots appeared to be of superior quality. They maintained the American formation, flying and fighting in two-plane

approaching Bhamo, at which point I was able to put my plane in a slight dive, in which I outdistanced the enemy. The Tojos broke off the action and I turned back, climbing and attempted to resume the engagement. Climbing to 1,500ft [457m] to the southeast of Bhamo, I saw a formation of four Tojos in two elements of two planes each.

"The two elements divided right and left and turned to attack me from both sides. I attempted violent evasive action and with two Tojos on my tail in a steep climb, my engine seemed to explode. I increased my angle of dive, evaded the enemy, and landed at Bhamo II landing ground at 1500hrs.

Hammer's wingman, Lt. Howarth claimed one more Japanese aircraft destroyed: "I first noticed violent evasive action on the part of the C-47 which had completed its dropping activities. At this moment, Lt. Hammer dived sharply and I followed him down, dropping my wing tanks when I saw his fall. I blacked out for a moment in a fast turn and when I recovered consciousness, I saw one Tojo, which had turned into Lt. Hammer, coming towards me. We were then 1,000ft [305m] above the mountains. I succeeded in getting into the blind spot of this Tojo and as he pulled up in a slight bank, I commenced firing and pressed the attack closely. Strikes were noted on the fuselage, large pieces flew off the cockpit of the Tojo, and the plane started in a steep dive on its back.

Above: In addition to P-47s, the 80th Fighter Group's 459th Fighter Squadron also flew P-38s. Combat operations for the 80th effectively ceased by May 1945 and the group was withdrawn from theater.

elements. They were aggressive and showed excellent control of their planes. They avoided head-on passes, concentrating their attacks on the rear. At deck altitude, the Tojo could apparently gain on a P-47 in level flight, in spite of War Emergency Power. However, the P-47 quickly outdistanced the Tojo in a slight dive. The P-47 at high speed appeared to be able to turn inside the Tojo, but no engagement was pressed sufficiently to make this point certain."

Mission Peculiarities

Lt. Robert Dennison, 60th Fighter Squadron, explained what it was like both to live and to fight in the CBI Theater, and handle some troublesome flight issues. "We lived on an old tea plantation. The thatch-roofed residence was our Officers' Mess. Our quarters were bamboo Bashas and we slept under mosquito netting while our shoes turned moldy from the perpetual dampness. Several guys came down with malaria in spite of the Atabrine tablets that we were required to take daily. The war was in Burma to the south of Assam. Our mission was mainly close support of ground troops. We also dive-bombed and strafed bridges and airfields, most of which were now abandoned.

"We moved to a new base in northern Burma, called Sahmaw, as soon as the ground forces had pushed the Japs far enough south [December 26, 1944]. While there, my squadron set a theater record for the most sorties flown. Each of us would frequently fly two or three missions a day. On the 29th of December 1944, I personally flew four sorties.

"One incident I recall occurred on a big mission when we were launching sixteen P-47s. Each of us carried two 500lb [227kg] bombs and of course, our eight .50-caliber machine guns, fully loaded plus a full load of fuel. We were pretty heavy. I was element leader of the second flight of four and the squadron commander was leading the mission. With that many airplanes involved, the procedure called for fairly close interval takeoffs and the leader would

Above: Propeller upgrade. This earlier camouflaged 33rd Fighter Group Thunderbolt is having a new "symmetric" Curtiss Electric 836-14C2-1081 propeller installed, which will increase both rate of climb and top speed.

Left: Both the 33rd and 311th Fighter Groups called Pungchacheng airfield home from the end of 1944 through the cessation of hostilities
Below: GIs in the sweltering Burma heat often purchased British uniform shorts or similar locally produced shorts for some relief from the heat.

circle the field until all of the aircraft were off the ground and had joined up in formation before he would set course for the target.

"I had just taken off and was about to join up on my flight leader when I noticed that my airspeed indicator read zero! I immediately looked at my pitot tube on the leading edge of the [left] wing and saw the canvas cover still installed. Both my crew chief and I had failed to check this before I climbed into the cockpit. Since the airspeed indicator is one of the primary instruments in case you encounter bad weather, I figured this could be a serious problem. I called the CO and advised him of my problem and requested instructions. He told me to land, remove the pitot cover, and take off again. He would circle the field and wait for me.

"At Sahmaw, there was a hill off the north end of the runway so we always took off to the south and landed to the north, regardless of the wind condition. The last airplane had just taken off, so I flew a semi-normal approach to

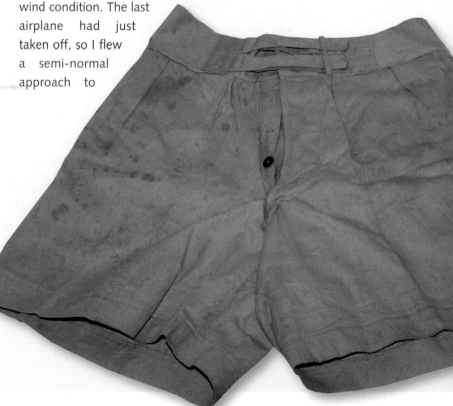

Above: (L to R) Lt. S. R. Jenkins, Col. Philip Klein, and Lt. Dee Finley flew the first three Thunderbolts into China, landing at Kunming Airfield on April 20, 1944.

Right: A local artisan-produced bullion-thread-on-velvet CBI shoulder patch.

land. Normal meant diving at the approach end of the runway to a very low altitude (like ten feet!), then pitching up and left into a tight 360 degree turn while lowering the landing gear and flaps. The final approach would be a descending turn right down to the runway where you would level your wings and touch down at about the same time. These hotshot approaches were strictly forbidden in the States, but overseas we could get away with it.

"Since I had no airspeed indicator to refer to and was much heavier than I had ever been for landing, I wanted to make my approach as much as I could like I was used to doing it. I succeeded in making a pretty good approach by the seat of my pants, but I landed hot to avoid stalling. I had to stand on the brakes and got stopped with only a few feet of runway left. My crew chief was waiting for me and removed the pitot tube cover. I quickly turned the airplane around and took off again, joined the formation and went dive-bombing. I had caused a delay of six of seven minutes, so I was somewhat embarrassed, but a lot wiser. I never failed to check my pitot tube for the rest of my flying career!"

Thunderbolt I and II — Royal Air Force Thunderbolts in the CBI

The RAF required a capable aircraft to replace the aging Hurricane, which had been the mainstay fighter-bomber in Burma, but needed an aircraft capable of performing the bomber escort mission as well. With Hawker focused on providing enough Typhoons to meet ETO fighter-bomber requirements, the RAF needed another solution. Through Lend-Lease the RAF began to receive Thunderbolts in the late spring 1944, and No. 135 Squadron was the first to turn in their Hurricane IIs for the new fighter. No. 135 Squadron flew their first combat mission toward the end of May 1944 and more squadrons followed through the summer. In all, fifteen RAF squadrons flew the Thunderbolt in the CBI Theater. The most common mission profile flown by RAF Thunderbolts was "Cab Rank": on-call close air support for frontline ground units. The standard load for such a mission was three 500lb (227kg) GP bombs. As with US Thunderbolt units (procedures were built from the first US squadrons flying with the RAF in North Africa), RAF squadrons would get a briefing of the ground situation, take off, and then check in with the forward ground controller. The Cab Rank controller would then vector them to the highest-priority target. The RAF was the second largest operator of the Thunderbolt, with 851 airframes ordered by war's end. The first 232 airplanes accepted in to service were P-47D-21 and D-22-RE Razorback models and were designated the Thunderbolt Mk I. The remainder were a mix of Farmingdale-built P-47D-25, -27, -28 and -30s; designated Thunderbolt Mk II.

Above: Two Royal Air Force Thunderbolt Mark IIs (KJ140 'RS-B' and HD265 'RS-G') of No. 30 Squadron RAF being serviced at Jumchar, India. A B-29 Superfortress sits impressively in the background.

Ground-Crew Roles

"Japanese opposition was not the only enemy. In the dense jungles temperatures sometimes soared to 140° and the humidity hovered near 100 percent. Crews worked amidst swarms of beetles, flies, and gnats. At night, sleeping required the use of mosquito netting."

—Sgt. Walter Contreras, 90th Fighter Squadron

There is an old adage in combat units that pilots don't own their planes, they just borrow them from their crew chief for a bit. Each fighter squadron was divided into sections focusing on specific aspects of the airplane. The crew chief fell under the squadron engineering section. He and his assistant crew chief dealt with airframe and powerplant maintenance and repair.

The armament section was responsible not just for the Jug's eight .50-caliber guns, but also the functionality of the airplane's gunsight and its proper boresighting. In addition, the armament team made sure each airplane had the proper collimation of those eight guns to converge at a point in space, usually 300yd (274m) in front of the airplane. The force of eight .50-caliber machine guns converging on a single point the size of a dinner plate had the equivalent force of being hit by a freight train at full steam: the effects of a properly collimated P-47 burst were devastating. The armament crews were also responsible for loading the maximum 425-round belts of .50-caliber ammunition into each of the Thunderbolt's eight guns.

Lastly, the ordnance section focused on identifying, assembling, transporting, and loading the various types of munitions carried by the P-47 on a combat mission. Once the mission order was given, with the specific weapon types, the ordnance section jumped into action, ensuring the proper ordnance was allocated for all aircraft participating in the mission. The ordnance section used the Chevrolet M6 bomb service truck and M5 bomb trailer to transport the squadron's ordnance from the bomb dump to the flightline.

The ground crews were usually the fighter squadron's innovators. If a problem came up, USAAF ground crews were the best at engineering a solution. In the CBI, when the 81st Fighter Group was operating on reduced quantities of purified water, men of the armament and engineering sections built their own water purifiers, as the central supply was inadequate for the thirsty crews and armament men. As a result, both sections turned out excellent records in keeping the Thunderbolts ready to fly. The extreme dust conditions added a handicap to their work, but with their engineered solution, there was no reduction in operational readiness.

In the 333rd Fighter Squadron, a new life raft carrier was designed by armament NCOs SSgt. Harold W. Fox and Sgt. Robert B. Cherrier. The two used a 15-gal (57-liter) water barrels and a 75-gallon (284-liter) belly tank. The new carrier, which was streamlined, promised to increase the efficiency of the P-47 carrying it on

Left: Sgt. Jack Kubler (in cockpit), Sgt. Anton Hrna (on box), Lt. William Terranova (kneeling on wing), and Cpl. Robert Bowers are boresighting eight .50-caliber machine guns to converge at a specific point in space in front of the Thunderbolt.

Rescue Combat Air Patrol (RESCAP) missions searching for aircrews who had ditched en route back to Okinawa. Both NCOs were awarded the Bronze Star Medal for their innovation, one that improved the survival chances of aircrews downed in the waters around the Ryukyus.

On Ie Shima, difficulties were encountered performing maintenance on the 333rd Fighter Squadron's aircraft. Due to the fact that this was the first time the P-47N was used in combat, several bugs were encountered. The most serious trouble was engines cutting out on takeoff. Investigations revealed no specific causes other than the fact that the runway was too short to get the P-47N off with full external fuel

Above: *Precisely collimating the eight .50-caliber machine guns, the P-47 ground crew made the airplane a far more effective weapon of war, as Thunderbolt pilots could better observe the effects of their rounds as they pulled into range.*

loads and War Emergency Power. However the same investigation also looked into several landing gear collapses and found that dust covers on the landing gear down locks proved to be insufficient. Dirt and coral dust accumulated in the down lock latches, preventing the landing gear from locking in the down position. Daily inspections and a considerable amount of cleaning remedied this condition. Eventually the Thunderbolts of all three groups on Ie Shima got new, locally produced leather covers to better protect the locking mechanisms from dirt and dust.

With the introduction of the K-14 gyroscopic gunsight on late model P-47Ds, Ms, and Ns, the armament sections now had to maintain a precision instrument designed to compute a firing solution for the pilot. The 73rd Fighter Squadron on Ie Shima initially had some difficulty with

Above: *Sgts. John Koval and Joe DiFranza loading .50-caliber ammunition for Lt. Col. Francis Gabreski's P-47D-25-RE in the summer of 1944. Each belt had to be placed precisely into the ammunition trough to prevent binding of the belt.*

the sights. "The armament and ordnance sections are well organized and have adequate facilities. Modifications were made during the month on .50-caliber machine guns and on the gyro-gunsight wiring. These gyro-gunsights were difficult to keep in good working order due to the lack of replacement parts. The old Mk. 8 gunsight, which many of the pilots seem to favor over the gyro sight, was installed in two of the planes."

Jungle Rescue

While combat over Europe was usually fought over a relatively developed countryside, and in the Pacific it was either over open water or fairly small islands, Burma presented a different problem: vast stretches of dense jungle and extremely remote areas. If a pilot went down, it could take weeks or months to get back to his unit, if the jungle didn't kill him first. The two liaison squadrons assigned to the 1st Air Commando Group were tasked with Combat Search and Rescue (CSAR), and as Capt. William Hemphill, CO of the 6th Fighter Squadron (Commando) found out firsthand on April 17, 1945, they were critical to the survival of downed aviators.

"Our mission was to dive-bomb Thaungdainggon, a small village 5 miles [8km] south of Toungoo, Burma. I made my bombing dive at 0940hrs to the north, released at a safe altitude, and was making a climbing turn to the left when I felt a jolt at about 4,000ft [1,219m]. I believe I was hit by ground fire, although I did not see any flashes or tracers. The engine began to backfire and miss. I pushed the mixture

Above: The lack of airfield support vehicles occasionally pressed local infrastructure into service as a result. Here a civilian fuel trailer is pulled by a team of oxen in order to assist refueling 1st Air Commando Group Thunderbolts.

control to full-rich and checked the gas selector cock, but the missing continued and oil started to come out of the left side of the engine.

"I called 'Hemphill to flight, will have to belly in. Go get an L-5.' I had hoped to get enough power to get back across the British lines but suddenly oil covered the whole canopy. Other pilots told me that a column of black smoke a mile long was trailing behind me. Although the

squadron had set a procedure for such an emergency, I wasn't taking any chances and I called a second time: 'Hemphill to James, Go to Meiktila and get an L-5.' We had a light plane squadron based at Meiktila for evacuating casualties.

"I opened the canopy and from the side I could see level land ahead. There was a tree in my path, but I didn't see it because there was oil all over my canopy. I was indicating about 130 when I felt a terrific jolt. That was when I hit the tree. The canopy slammed shut and the plane skidded to a stop about 30yd [27m] beyond. The engine was hissing and billowing smoke out to the left. Fire broke out immediately and was coming out of the cowl flaps and reached the wing roots. I tried to open the canopy, but it was stuck. The jettison release wouldn't work. After about thirty seconds that seemed like thirty minutes, I got the canopy open far enough to put my elbows in the opening on either side and shoved the canopy all the way back. I climbed out on the wing and started to reach back into the cockpit for some things I might need: cap, jacket, maps, carbine, and ammunition. Flames were now licking around my feet and I gave up the idea of trying to get anything out of the plane.

"Then I got out my cloth map and proceeded to check my position and the direction I would follow. Before landing I had formulated a plan to keep to the high grass and brush and walk to the north and slightly west where I would hit the closest friendly troops. I knew my position to be a few miles southwest of Toungoo.

"My leg had been cut when it struck the oxygen instrument panel. I put a hasty bandage on my leg and then started to walk. Soon I came to a hiding place and I stopped to put another bandage on. I had perspired so much that my coveralls, shorts, and socks were completely drenched and the adhesive tape I had used on the bandage had not stuck. I shook sulpha powder on the cut and tied on a new bandage. I checked my supplies, finding I had several chocolate bars, some canned rations, medical supplies including atabrine and halazone, a map, compass, signal mirror, pistol, extra socks, and a canteen of water. I was terribly thirsty having lost so much perspiration. I wanted water in the worst way, but I wouldn't take any for fear I would be tempted to take too much. I figured it would be at least 1230hrs before an L-5 could get back, and I was determined not to touch any until the L-5 arrived. Time passed slowly, and then at about 1230hrs I saw two P-47s weaving and then I saw that they were escorting two L-5s.

"I came out into the open and ran back to my plane. As I got nearer, I could see a group of natives around the plane. Then I saw a Jap, rifle in hand, running away from the L-5 that was about to land. He also was running with his back to me, which excited me. I threw a cartridge in to

The natives along with Capts. Davis and Hemphill freed the airplane and pushed it to the end of a flat run of ground. Dropping the flaps and revving to maximum power, Davis and Hemphill were able to get off the ground and fly to Meiktila. Incidents like Capt. Hemphill's three hours on the ground were a rare occurrence, but the availability of rescue aircraft like the L-5 foreshadowed the evolution in technology that would develop CSAR in the subsequent decades.

Top: A Jungle Survival Kit. The contents include a US flag, map, compass, currency, a magnifying glass, and a "blood chit" explaining the pilot's situation.
Above: 1st Air Commando Thunderbolts all carried the group's distinctive five diagonal bands around the rear fuselage.

the chamber of my pistol. He continued to run and I didn't shoot. The L-5 landed in a rice paddy just north of my plane. It stopped with its wheels in a ditch, nose-down. Fortunately the propeller was horizontal and was not damaged. The tail wheel was broken, but there was no other apparent damage although the plane had received a severe jolt.

"The pilot, Capt. Frank Davis, and I tried to push the plane, but we couldn't budge it. The pilot of the second L-5 dropped a note telling us to hide while he went and got more help. I didn't like the idea of waiting, especially after seeing the Jap and thought we ought to make every effort to get it off. If we failed, we would still be no worse off than we were on that ground. I called to the natives and made them understand that we wanted them to help push."

Above: 1st Air Commando Thunderbolts strafe Japanese positions around Meiktila, Burma, while Commonwealth troops of the British 17th Division appreciate and observe the effects.

Speed Demons

*"I singled out one Me 109F who tried to turn and climb,
but it was useless, as I could outclimb him with the M-1
Model employing 75in [191cm][of manifold pressure].
The enemy aircraft then spiraled down. For a while I had
to throttle back as to not overrun him.*

—Maj. Paul Conger, CO 63rd Fighter Squadron, January 14, 1945

The P-47M mated the new R2800C series engine with the P-47D-30 airframe, and the resulting combination became the fastest Thunderbolt variant, topping out at 480mph (772kmh) in level flight using War Emergency Power. The first P-47M-1-REs arrived in England in December 1944 and were immediately assigned to the 56th Fighter Group's three squadrons. Yet despite the new airplane's stunning speed, the type almost immediately ran into mechanical issues, resulting in loss of power and complete engine failures in the early weeks of 1945. Maj. Paul Conger was the first pilot to score with the P-47M-1-RE in combat, but the group's M models would remain grounded throughout February 1945, while the engine failure cause was determined. After an exhaustive investigation, it was discovered that the ignition harnesses on the new C-series engines were brittle and cracking and would eventually fail in flight.

In addition to the wiring harness issues, the higher operating temperatures and pressures of the new engines caused internal damage that would quickly lead to engine failures. The immediate cause was due to corrosion within the cylinder walls, due to improper preparation for overseas shipment, but the problems ran deeper. With the number of engine failures increasing through January

Left: "Josephine my Flying Machine" was 2nd Lt. Leo Butiste's P-47M. He claimed a single-engine aircraft and an He 111 destroyed on a April 10, 1945, strafing mission to Werder airfield.

1945, the 56th Fighter Group, 8th Air Force, and Republic Aircraft began an investigation to determine the causes. Of the eighteen engines that failed, all had burnt pistons, indicating severe temperatures and pressures and a lack of water injection for cooling purposes. It was discovered that during each engine's testing phase before acceptance, they had been run with intermittent water injection at a constant high-power setting, resulting in some damage to the pistons. It was also speculated, but never proven, that Pratt & Whitney changed the materials used in the R2800C's pistons and rings.

According to the Air Technical Service Command, "All War Emergency Power operation on the R-2800C engine should be with a mixture of 25% Ethyl alcohol, 25% Methyl alcohol, and 50% water to prevent piston failures due to detonation. Action has been taken to inform the 8th Air Force that no War Emergency Power should be utilized without the specified methanol/water mixture." Once the faulty engines were replaced, the group was able to resume operations with the new fighter. But until all of the M models were cleared, the 56th retained their P-47Ds for combat.

By early March 1945, the 8th Air Force's sole P-47 fighter group was back to flying combat missions over Europe. Carrying a standard load of either two or three 210-gal (795-liter) drop tanks, the 56th's P-47Ms now had the range to reach as far as the P-51.

First Kill for the M Model

The P-47M's first kill came in mid-January 1945, nearly two months before the entire 56th Fighter Group had transitioned to the M model, and before all of the new type's bugs were worked out. Yet Maj. Paul Conger flew his new mount "Bernyce" (P-47M-1-RE serial number 44-21134) on a mission on January 14, 1945, during which he expended more than 1,200 rounds of .50-caliber machine-gun ammunition and claimed the type's first victory.

"I was flying as Fairbanks leader, leading Daily Squadron. We reached our area at 1150hrs SE of Luneburg at 28,000ft [8,534m]. Made a turn approximately 030, sweeping largely around Schwerner Lake, east of Parchim, where at 1220hrs Big Friends [US bombers] were seen coming in to the territory from Hamburg NW of us. We crossed their path in front, flying about 180 degrees. Mustang flights were visual near Stendal. Platform Squadron, which were wide on my left, encountered thirty-plus Me 109s at 1245hrs, which had made definite attacks on the Mustangs coming down from an altitude of 35,000ft [10,668m] or so.

By the time I got over there, all of the Me 109s were in singles, dog fighting, spirals, etc. with the Mustangs at 23,000ft [7,010m] to the deck. I singled out one Me 109F who tried to turn and climb, but it was useless, as I could outclimb him with the M-1 Model employing 75in [191cm]. The enemy aircraft then spiraled down. For a while I had to throttle back as to not overrun him. The Jerry would climb, his rate of roll being better, but my turn and climb had me constantly overrunning him at a 40-degree angle. I finally saw hits on the tip of his wing as he rolled out straight. Unfortunately I had hit my gun switch to off, so my spurt was useless. At this time, we were at 8,000ft [2,438m] and the enemy aircraft split-S'd, pulled out, and I lost him on the deck. I claim this 109 damaged.

Right: While the "bugs" were worked out of the group's P-47Ms, they continued flying missions in their D models, like twenty-one-kill ace Capt. Fred Christensen's "Rozzie Geth/Miss Fire," a P-47D-25-RE.

Left: Lt Edmund Ellis of the 61st Fighter Squadron stands on the wing of his P-47M "Blue Eyes," in March 1945. His airplane was coded HV-T and was painted semi-gloss black with metal undersides.

"As I climbed back up to 12,000ft [3,658m], three Me 109s attacked me from 3 o'clock. I spiraled, climbed to 27,000ft [8,230m] at 160mph [257km/h], easily pulling away from the enemy aircraft at 75in [91cm]. Keeping their deflection angle high, I peeled back down on the tail end Me 109 at 15,000ft [4,572m]. The three diving enemy aircraft bounced two Mustangs. I closed in on the third to about 400yd [366m]. I gave him a spurt, hitting his under-fuselage, wing roots, as glycol poured out and pieces flew off of his right wing. His canopy flew off as he went into a spiral to the right. The pilot did not bail out. But after the third time of the spiral, the enemy aircraft burst into flames all over as it went into a more pronounced dive straight down."

Right: *The khaki cotton webbing with aluminum fittings was what kept a Thunderbolt pilot in his seat.*

numerous strikes all over his canopy. Immediately after I stopped firing, the enemy aircraft went into a quick, tight uncontrollable spin, leaving a trail of white smoke behind him. I made another orbit, one of the P-51s joined our flight and we came out together."

1st Lt. David Magel's flight was providing top cover and was able to confirm Trumble's kills. "About 2,000ft [610m] below us, I saw two P-51s engaged with four Me 109s, so we went down on the enemy aircraft. I saw Lt. Trumble firing on one of the enemy aircraft and observed several strikes before it went into a spin and burst into flames about 8,000ft [2,438m]. Out of the remaining three Me 109s, two of them hit the deck, but the other remained in a Lufberry. Again, Lt. Trumble singled out this remaining aircraft and opened fire. I observed several strikes about the enemy aircraft's canopy and finally the canopy came off, along with several pieces of metal from the side of the ship, just below the windshield. It went into a spin and I lost sight of it, but it was definitely out of control."

Above: *Maj. Paul Conger's "Bernyce" drew first blood for the P-47M on January 14, 1945, with Conger shooting down an Me 109 and damaging another over Parchim.*

Lt. Pershing Trumble leading Red Flight in a P-47D-25-RE also claimed another Me 109 on the 14th: "We were flying at 25,000ft [7,620m], approaching Stendal at approximately 1245hrs when our squadron came upon a big dog fight in that vicinity between twenty-five plus Me 109s and some P-51s. Due to an early return, our flight consisted of only three men. With End Flight staying up for top cover, we started down to engage the enemy. We picked out four Me 109s that were engaged with two p-51s. Two of the enemy planes split-S'd for the deck. I closed in and turned with one of the enemy aircraft, getting a 45-degree deflection. I poured my lead into him and observed many strikes hitting his aircraft. "The enemy aircraft began to go down in a large slow spiral and when he got to about 10,000ft [3,048m], the plane exploded in the air, bursting into flames at the same time. I did not see any chute and don't see how the pilot could have bailed out. I did a 360-degree, found another 109, singled him out, and closed in on him. I fired a few short bursts and saw

Above: *Maj. Conger, CO of the 63rd Fighter Squadron, along with Lts. Cameron Hart and Philip Kuhn, standing in front of one of the squadron's P-47D-25s.*

Flying Fighter Cover over Remagen

With the US First Army successfully holding the Remagen bridgehead over the Rhine River in the spring of 1945, the Luftwaffe tried desperately to destroy both the Ludendorff Bridge and the American pontoon bridges established alongside it. A ring of American anti-aircraft artillery (AAA) was emplaced around the bridgehead, but fighter cover was still a critical element in the bridgehead's defense. Careful coordination was critical during intercepts over the bridge, as eager AAA gunners weren't always careful to distinguish friend from foe, and the intercepts often occurred at medium to low altitude; well within the engagement range of those gunners on the ground.

On March 10, the 62nd Fighter Squadron broke up a mixed formation of Fw 190s and Me 109s headed for the target area. Lt. Norman Gould was leading the second element in Platform White Flight and claimed the first enemy aircraft of the day: "I was flying Platform White Three on the mission of March 10 to Remagen to defend the bridge there. We arrived at 1520hrs. After arriving in the target area, we patrolled for about ten minutes. At this time, I called in a formation of six 109s heading north. We made a 180-degree turn on their tail and my wingman, Lt. Ducey, White Four, got in a very good position so I called him to fire and that I would fly his wing. He fired from line astern from 300yd [274m], down to 100yd [91m], getting numerous strikes. The aircraft went into a cloud and we lost sight of him. I called him to fly on me and I bounced another Me 109 that made cloud cover before

Below: After ten days of military vehicles crossing it, the Ludendorff Bridge at Remagen collapsed. However, by that point US First Army had already established a significant beachhead on the Rhine's east bank.

I could reach firing range. At this time, two Me 109s came out of a cloud going 90 degrees to me at 1,500ft [457m]. I rolled into the last one and fired a short burst from approximately 400yd [366m], which hit him in the cockpit. He rolled over on his back and hit the ground in an inverted 40-degree dive and exploded.

"As I recovered from my half-roll, I saw an Fw 190 bounce me from the clouds. I broke left and I saw Blue Leader, Lt. Henley and White Two, Lt. Carroll getting strikes on this Fw 190 from opposite sides. The Jerry pulled up, apparently in an attempt to reach cloud cover, when he bailed out."

A good flight lead knows when his wingman is in a better position to fire on the enemy, and so Gould directed Lt. David Ducey to engage: "I was flying White Four on March 10 when we spotted six Me 109s. We broke into them and since I was in good position, my element leader told me to fire. I began to fire and saw some hits on one of them before they pulled up into the clouds and disappeared. White Three then called me and asked that I fly his wing again. Two Me 109s came out of the clouds. Lt. Gould began firing at one. I saw hits on the 109's canopy after which it did a split-S, hit the ground, and exploded."

1st Lt. Donald Henley was leading the squadron's Blue Flight and arrived over the target area about ten minutes after Lt. Gould's flight, witnessing their kills and scoring another. "I was Platform Blue Leader on the mission to defend the bridge at Remagen from Jerry dive-bombers. We reached the area about 1530hrs and stooged south when six Me 109s tried to join our formation. We turned with them as a

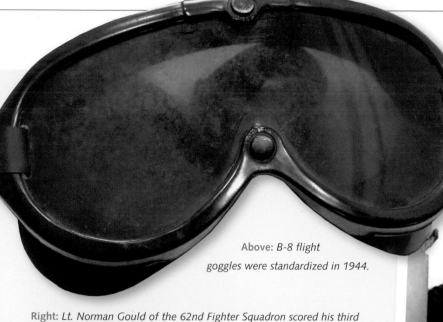

Above: B-8 flight goggles were standardized in 1944.

Right: Lt. Norman Gould of the 62nd Fighter Squadron scored his third confirmed kill on March 10, 1945, over the Remagen bridgehead.

Above: Lt. Luther Hines was killed as a result of a mid-air training accident in March 1945. His P-47M collided with newly arrived Lt. Richard Tuttle's airplane during a cross-over formation practice.

squadron, but the 109s gave it the liquid oxygen and jettisoned their bombs and turned into the clouds. I turned inside of platform leader and cut them off and almost had a mid-air collision with the leading 109 and platform leader. The 109s climbed into the clouds and disappeared.

"We stooged around waiting for them to come down when I heard Lt. Gould say that he hit a 109 and I looked to my left and saw an Me 109 and an Fw 190 split-S'ing from about 2,000ft [610m]. The 109 hit the ground and burned. The Fw 190 got away. I then saw an Fw 190 pop out of the clouds in front of me and in line astern of Lt. Gould. I started after him and Lt. Carroll, White Two, was seen to be on the Jerry's tail. I

pulled up in a steep right climbing turn and fired, observing strikes all over the right side of the 190. The pilot bailed out and the Fw 190 crashed and burned. I went down after the pilot, but he had already hit the ground and was running for cover. I think that Platform White Two, Lt. Carroll nailed him."

Lt. Carroll, flying Lt. Henley's wing was also able to confirm Lt. Gould's second kill as Blue Flight arrived over the target area: "I was flying Platform White Two and we were flying just under a cloud layer which was at 3,500–4,000ft [1,067–1,219m] when an Fw 190 popped out of the clouds and bounced White Three, Lt. Gould. White Three immediately broke left and the Jerry fired at him. He wasn't able to get any deflection and reversed his turn, pulled up into a steep chandelle, doing two rolls, when I got on his tail and fired at no deflection and very close range (approx 100yd [91m]). I noticed strikes all over the plane and it started to break up. The pilot bailed out, his chute opening."

Below: Once the engine power loss issues were fixed, the P-47M was an outstanding airplane to fly in combat, but those early sorties resulted in a higher than normal crash rate. Here we see one unfortunate aircraft being recovered.

Facing the Jets!

March 1945 would be the 56th Fighter Group's most successful month against German jets, with a total of four destroyed. The 56th would claim two more Me 262s in April and would finish as the top jet-killing Thunderbolt unit of the war. Although the 56th Fighter Group shared one of the first Me 262 kills in November 1944, the group did not score against any jet aircraft between November 12 and March 14, 1945. The group's jet drought ended in a big way on March 14, however, when the 62nd Fighter Squadron encountered three Ar 234s of KG76 near Coblenz, destroying two of them. Lt. Warren Lear caught the first Ar 234 unaware and sent it spiraling earthward:

"I was flying Platform Blue Three at 20,000ft [6,096m] northeast of Coblenz when three bogeys were called in. I saw them at 1030hrs to 11 o'clock high—someone called them in as A-20s, but I saw the German

Right: 62nd Fighter Squadron CO, Maj. Mike Jackson getting into the cockpit of his P-47M.

him. Lt. Hall, Platform Blue Leader, closed in from 6 o'clock and got in a long burst on him. The jet [pilot] released his canopy and bailed out. I was behind him firing when he bailed out. The jet spun twice and then went straight in."

Above: The German Ar 234 (seen destroyed behind the Me 108 in the foreground) was the world's first jet bomber. Although it was only marginally faster than piston engine aircraft of its day, the 234 was a potent aircraft nonetheless.

crosses on the fuselage, the cross being black on a white background. I dropped my tanks and turned approximately 10 to 15 degrees to the right and was directly behind one of them and set my K-14 for a span of 42ft [13m]. I opened fire at approximately 700yd [640m] and got strikes on both jets and the left one started to burn, the right one smoking badly. I fired two more bursts and registered strikes all over the jet. I cut back on power and rpm as I was overshooting him. Pieces were falling off of the jet. I was overshooting and cut back and S'd behind and below

Lt. Norman Gould in the cover flight claimed his fourth kill on this mission when he outmaneuvered one of the Arados: "I was flying Platform Red Three when a flight of three jet Ar 234s passed over us in the Coblenz area. Blue Flight made the initial attack and our flight turned to give them support. At this time, two of the enemy aircraft were coming down in a shallow dive pressing an attack on my wingman, Platform Red 4. I immediately called him to break left, which he did. The Jerry did likewise, still attacking, however the turn put me in perfect position. I started to clobber him and noticing that he was being fired upon, the Jerry turned on his jets, but by that time, I was rapidly closing from approximately 300yd [274m] to point blank range at 15,000ft [4,571m] and observing strikes all the time. His right engine was enveloped in flames and the enemy aircraft proceeded to spin earthward. He exploded upon impact, no chutes were observed."

Eleven days later, the 63rd Fighter Squadron engaged Me 262s of JG7 attacking the bomber stream. Capt. George Bostwick was flying P-47M 44-21160 "Devastatin' Deb" when he bounced one of the attacking 262s. "I was leading Daily Squadron on an escort mission in the vicinity of Hamburg. We were on the right and to the rear of our box of bombers when my Red Leader called in several bogies closing rapidly on a small group of bombers at about 8 o'clock to us. There were about fifteen bombers in this group. They were in a good formation, but were some distance away from the rest of their box. I turned toward them just in time to see two bombers explode. The enemy aircraft (Me 262s) split up after their attack, most of them heading roughly east. I followed them until I lost sight of them and then proceeded to look over all of the airfields in the area. I finally found the airdrome at Parchim and orbited it at about 12,000ft [3,657m] for about twenty minutes. There were between twenty to thirty aircraft visible on the field. After many wide orbits, my number four man called in a bogie and I directed him to lead off. This enemy aircraft was also an Me 262 and he led us back to the airdrome. Upon approaching the airdrome, I spotted four more Me 262s milling around the airdrome almost on the deck. I picked out one who was flying parallel to the landing strip as if he might be going to peel off to land. He did not, however, but flew straight down the runway. As he reached the end of the runway, he passed over a second enemy aircraft, which was taking off and was just breaking the ground. I pulled my nose

Left: The "pinks" overseas cap was not an issue piece of headgear, but it looked sharp on fighter pilots.

attacked by eight jets (Me 262s) and we took out after them. They outran us, but we ran across an airdrome that had twenty to thirty twin-unit jets on it. As we circled the airdrome at about 12,000ft [3,657m], I saw a bogie in the distance at 3 o'clock level. I was told to take out after it, which I did. It was in a dive, coming toward me at about a 45-degree angle off my right. As I turned toward him, he turned away from me and I could not catch him. While still considerably out of range, he started a medium

Above: On April 7, 1945, Capt. George Bostwick shot down a pair of Me 109s and damaged an Me 262 over Bremen, bringing his total to eight confirmed kills.

Above: Maj. Jackson's P-47M-1-RE 44-21117. On March 14, Lt. Sherman Pruitt shot down an Me 109 in this airplane after a lengthy chase.

through to get a shot at this enemy aircraft, but before I could, he apparently saw me and made a tight turn to the left. His left wing dug into the ground and the plane cart-wheeled, breaking into many pieces and strewing wreckage for some distance."

Lt. Edwin Crosthwaite claimed the second jet of the day: "I was flying Number 4 in Daily Squadron White Flight consisting of Capt. Bostwick, Lts. Hoffman, V. Smith, and myself. We were flying close escort to 2nd Division B-24s along with two groups of P-51s. The bombers were

turn to the left, thus giving me a chance to close. I was closing rapidly at approximately 5,000ft [1,524m] in the inside of the turn and fired two short bursts without hits. When I was about 50yd [457m] from him, he levelled out. That put me right in trail and I opened fire, observing strikes immediately and the right jet started to smoke. I fired until I overran him and pulled up and to the right. As I was in this position, I observed the canopy come off and the pilot bail out. The plane then crashed and burned. The jet was camouflaged in two-tone green with red and blue bands encircling the fuselage about a yard from the empennage."

Entertainment in the War Zone

The most readily available form of entertainment for Thunderbolt pilots and crews was nightly movies provided by the United Services Organization (USO) or the Special Services (the entertainment branch of the US military). While feature films like *Woman of the Year* (1924) with Katherine Hepburn and Spencer Tracy were shown, the screenings also included newsreels and updates on the progress of the war in other theaters. Movies were a way to bring the squadron together without the stress of operational tempo performance. The men of the 79th Fighter Group, for example, made good use of the Augusteo Theater in downtown Naples while the group flew from Capodichino Airfield. The theater showed a nightly movie and occasionally had live stage shows as well.

Many squadrons formed their own sports teams or played pick-up baseball or basketball during downtime. Acquiring a ball through the

Left: USO troupes traveled all around the war zone, entertaining troops wherever they could. By the spring of 1945, one such troupe put on a show for the 358th Fighter Group.

USO was fairly simple and the handle from an ever-present broom was frequently pressed into service as a bat. Bases were easily created from items such as a uniform jacket or a folded tarp, and the game was on.

The 85th Fighter Squadron inter-departmental softball league was organized in April 1944 and consisted of six teams. Armament, engineering, and flightline all organized teams from within their own departments, while ops, S-2, and communications got together to form one, as did the orderly room, supply, and transportation. The officers made up the sixth team in the league. Departmental officers played with their own departments as a rule. In addition to the softball league, the 85th also formed a baseball team to compete against other units in the MTO. Tryouts were held on April 7, 1944, and the team's first game was on the 11th, resulting in a 3-0 win over one of the other squadrons in the 79th Fighter Group.

Below: Baseball was a common activity. Here the 78th Fighter Group team takes on another local challenger on September 19, 1944.

While baseball was the most prevalent sport as "America's pastime," basketball was also very popular, particularly in the European theater, where paved areas or hard floors were more common. In late 1944, the 9th Air Force formed a basketball league, which played through February 1945. According to the squadron history, "The 411th FS Basketball team won the XXIX TAC championship and thus won for themselves the chance to play in the finals of the 9th Air Force Tournament at Paris. There they lost a hard-fought battle to the 9th Air Force Headquarters, the score being 63-62. We aren't making any excuses for them, but had they had the opportunity to practice, we feel certain that they would have brought home the proverbial bacon."

Above: *Baseball, basketball, and volleyball were all regular pastimes when ground crews needed to unwind.*

Along with movies and sports came the occasional USO show. Celebrities like Bob Hope and Francis Langford toured near continually during the war to bring a little humor and levity to the troops. On August 12, 1944, Hope and Langford performed for a crowd of GIs at Owi airfield off the coast of New Guinea, in the 35th Fighter Group's area of operations. Three weeks later, on the other side of the world, the 78th Fighter Group was treated to a similar show at their base in Duxford, England. The show started at 1830hrs and was the second of three scheduled shows for crooner Bing Crosby that day. Crosby performed his first show at the 482nd Bomb Group's base in Alconbury, then headed to Duxford where he delivered a dinnertime show, and then moved on to Ridgewell in Essex for the 381st Bomb Group. The USO "Camp Shows" were a significant morale booster, particularly in the Southwest Pacific, where many GIs hadn't seen an American woman for over a year.

Starring role for the 57th

While watching movies was standard fare, the 57th Fighter Group was even given the opportunity to star in its own movie. Filmed in the same manner and by the same director and crew that did *Memphis Belle: A Story of a Flying Fortress* the previous year (released in 1944), filming took place on Corsica in the summer of 1944. Camera men and technicians supervised by Lt. Col. William Wyler, nephew of the founder of Universal Studios and one of Hollywood's top directors, roamed freely through the squadrons filming the various activities of the men. On the afternoon of August 9, 1944, the crew attempted to capture a twelve-ship formation of the 66th Fighter Squadron. Their cameras and

crew were put aboard a B-25, but the photographers found their intended task impractical; later on they filmed a four-ship formation with much better results. In addition, six planes from each squadron mounted special cameras for the specific purpose of shooting pictures of dive-bombing attacks and strafing runs on actual combat missions. The rumor was that the picture was to be ready for release in the States around February 1945, but with the war drawing to a rapid conclusion, Universal Studios did not want to release the film, shelving the project until the lackluster release of *Thunderbolt* in 1947, much to Wyler's and the 57th's dismay.

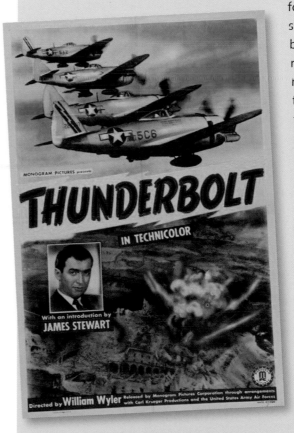

Above: *57th Fighter Group's VE Day celebration menu.*
Left: *Movie poster for the 1947 theatrical release of "Thunderbolt."*

Testing Out New Ammo!

The 56th Fighter Group launched a group-strength assault on Eggebek airfield on April 13, 1945, and caught between 150 and 200 airplanes on the ground. One of the key elements added to the mission was the new T48 high-velocity incendiary .50-caliber ammunition. The new ammo had a significantly higher muzzle velocity than the standard armor-piercing incendiary ammunition and therefore a flatter trajectory. Lt. Col. Lucian Dade, the group commander, led the mission and was the lead plane in the attack on the airfield.

Left: "Darling Dottie/Shoot you're faded" was the aircraft of Capt. Flagg, who destroyed two Fw 190s and a Ju 88 in this aircraft on April 13, 1945.
Right: The Luftwaffe Flak badge was awarded to all German antiaircraft gunners.

"The group made landfall in north of Hamburg and swept north to Eggebek airdrome as briefed at 1510hrs. The squadrons then took position with the 62nd top cover at 15,000ft [4,572m], 61st at 10,000ft [3,048m], and Blue Section of the 63rd with eight ships orbiting the field in string at 5,000ft [1,524m], and were to roll down to strafe any gun position that might open fire on either White or Red Flights. I was leading the White Section of the 63rd with eight ships and briefed these ships to make the initial flak run from south to north in an attempt to silence the known positions. The first pass was initiated from 9,000ft [2,743m] and hit the deck approximately 3 miles [5km] south of the field. Both flights were line abreast and indicating between 400 and 450mph [644 and 805kmh]. Three flak positions were identified and sprayed, but none seemed to be manned. Both flights continued on the deck to a point about 2 miles [3km] north of the aerodrome before recovering, White Flight to the left and Red Flight to the right. I received a hit by 20mm [fire] from a small village about 3 miles [5km] northwest of the aerodrome and also a .30-cal that seemed to be explosive. This gun position was not strafed as it could easily be avoided.

"There were an estimated 150–200 aircraft of all descriptions on the aerodrome and on two satellite fields, one to the north and one to the south. White and Red Flights of the 63rd Squadron again made passes from the south, concentrating on the southwest and northwest dispersals. After this pass and no serious flak was encountered, both Blue and Yellow Flights were called down to strafe.

"After five passes it was necessary for me to abort due to oil on my windshield and canopy. At this time only the 63rd Squadron was strafing and I counted 14 a/c destroyed. Seven were in the southwest dispersal, five in the northwest dispersal, and two along the hangar line.

"In all, this squadron made 140 individual passes, firing 31,148 rounds on the southwest, northwest, hangar line, and area north of the field

adjacent to the railroad. The area was so covered by smoke drifting from west to east that it was impossible to count individual fires. However, the two squadrons orbiting above estimated from forty to fifty as the 63rd left the aerodrome.

"The next squadron down was the 61st and their passes were made as follows: from southeast to northwest in the dispersal at the southwest corner. They then concentrated their passes on the northwest and northern area. Most of their passes were made on these two areas from south to north. This squadron made ninety-four individual passes, firing 22,243 rounds, and claimed twenty-five destroyed.

"This squadron made its first passes from northwest to southeast on the revetment area northwest of the field, then concentrated one flight

Above: Burning aircraft obscure the upper portion of this photo with thick black smoke at Werder Airdrome after a 56th Fighter Group strafing attack, three days prior to the attack on Eggebek.

Above: *Capt. Victor Bast (center) talking to his ground crew (l to r), Pvt Paul Innis, Sgt. Leon Hardy, crew chief Tech Sgt. Harold Keller and SSgt. Alvin Van Dorn.*

Above: *The reverse side of Capt. Flagg's P-47M-1-RE, 44-21140 aircraft.*

Right: *A hand-drawn map of Eggebek airdrome identifying the placement of all ninety-five enemy aircraft destroyed on the mission.*

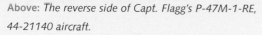

on the area adjacent to the railroad just to the northeast of the field while Blue Flight made passes on the area north of the aerodrome coming in north to south. At the same time, Yellow Flight was clearing the remainder of the northwest area and two planes on the field. The squadron made a total of 105 passes, expending 24,682 rounds, and claimed twenty-six aircraft destroyed."

Lt. Randel L. Murphy racked up an impressive ten enemy aircraft destroyed on this mission, setting a record for the most strafing kills on a single sortie. "While making approximately fifteen strafing passes on Eggebek airdrome and the adjoining fields, I observed at least thirty-five

to forty fires and explosions started by Daily Squadron. In a small field about 2 miles (3km) to the north, the enemy aircraft were parked practically wingtip to wingtip. All four sides of this field were lined with planes. To the south, on another small airfield, which had a grass runway outlined with white markers, there were at least twenty-plus enemy aircraft. More than one aircraft had been parked also in many of the revetments in the northwest part of the main airdrome. In most all instances, camouflage netting had been thrown over the aircraft, which carried the flames from one plane to another. Gas tanks, on exploding, would also spray the adjoining planes like phosphorous bombs. My guns were equipped with cal .50 high-velocity ammunition, T-48, and I noticed that the planes would burst into flames immediately upon securing strikes."

Murphy destroyed three He 111s, an Me 410, five unidentified twin-engine aircraft, and an Fw 200, plus damaged an Me 110, making him the top-scoring 8th Air Force strafing ace. Lt. Russell S. Kyler, also using the new T48 ammunition, accounted for five enemy aircraft that day. In all, the group claimed ninety-five aircraft destroyed and another ninety-five damaged, leaving no airplane on the field unscathed.

Jugs vs. Jets!

"As one started to attack my section from behind, I turned into him again and started firing head-on. He started to pull up and I pulled up with him and kept increasing my lead and firing long bursts as we closed. At the top of the pass, he fell off to the left and started down in a steep dive with heavy smoke pouring out of the fuselage."

—1st Lt. John Haun, 316th Fighter Squadron, April 4, 1945

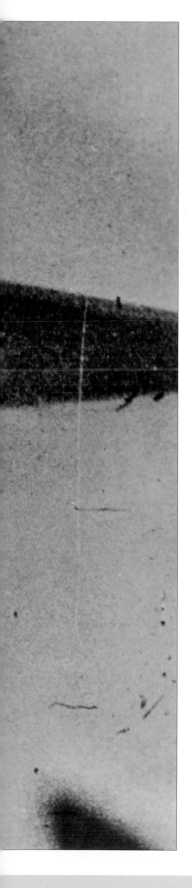

By August 1944, the Allied bombing effort was striking deeper into Germany than ever before. Allied armies were advancing across Europe at a breakneck pace and at mid-month, a second invasion of the European continent in southern France was dubbed the "Champagne Campaign," for the relatively light opposition encountered by the invasion force. The Allies were on the move and "home by Christmas" was the rumor of the day.

Yet the Germans, and the Luftwaffe in particular, were far from beaten in August when the first Me 262 jets were introduced into combat. The new airplane was a significant leap forward in aircraft technology, boasting a top speed of nearly 100mph (161km/h) faster than the P-47 and P-51. It was also heavily armed, with three 30mm MK108 cannons in the nose. One direct hit from a high-explosive 30mm round could easily destroy a single-engine fighter. Three or four hits could do the same to a four-engine bomber.

While the Me 262 had stunning performance, it was not without an Achilles' heel. The Jumo 004 engines that powered it were extremely temperamental and prone to

Left: Going down! A doomed Me 262 caught in an American fighter's gun camera. Although the Me 262 had superior speed compared to the P-47, the P-47 had a far better turning circle. An intelligent pilot could use this fact to good effect to bring the guns to bear at the right moment.

flaming out with abrupt changes in throttle settings, something that was critical to survival in air-to-air combat. Also, due to the lack of high-temperature alloys, the combustion chambers of the overly sensitive engines only had a useful service life of about eight hours before a complete change was necessary.

The first few encounters between the P-47 and Me 262 caught the jets at low altitude and airspeed either landing or taking off, when the jets were most vulnerable. However, as the war went on and encounters became more frequent, new tactics were developed to counter the "Schwalbe's" speed advantage. The 262 had an incredible rate of climb, but both the P-47 and P-51 found it very easy to turn inside the 262's immense turning arc and bring their guns to bear on the jets.

The P-51 Mustang scored significantly more kills against the Me 262 in combat, but that fact has more to do with the roles assigned to each type of fighter aircraft than with their actual performance. The P-51s were usually up where the 262s attacked bomber formations, while P-47s were usually down low attacking ground targets. The Mustangs simply had more opportunities to engage the Messerschmitt jet. However, when the P-47 was able to engage the 262, it held its own and usually came out on top. In all, US P-47s claimed twenty Me 262s and at least three Ar 234s destroyed between August 1944 and April 1945.

First Kills

Maj. Joseph Myers and Lt. Manford Croy, of the 82nd Fighter Squadron, scored the first confirmed kill against the new Me 262 on August 28, 1944. "While stooging around west of Brussels at 11,000ft [3,352m] I caught sight of what appeared to be a B-26 flying at about 500ft [152m] and heading in a southerly direction and going very fast. I immediately started down to investigate and although diving at 45-degrees and at 450 IAS [Indicated Airspeed], I was no more than holding my own in regard to the unidentified aircraft. When approximately 5,000ft [1,524ft] above and very nearly directly over the aircraft, I could see that it was not a B-26, although it had the general overall plan of a B-26. It was painted a slate blue color, with a long rounded nose, but I did not see any guns sticking out anyplace. It bore no markings. The unidentified plane must have seen me at this time, because at this point he started evasive action, which consisted of small changes of direction not exceeding 90 degrees of turn. The radius of turn was very great and although I was diving at around 450 IAS, I had very little trouble cutting him off and causing him again to change direction. He made no effort to climb or turn more than 90 degrees at any time. I closed to within 2,000ft [610m] above and directly astern of the aircraft and had full power on in a 45-degree dive in an effort to close. At this distance, I could readily see the similarity between the aircraft and the recognition plates of the Me 262. With full power on and the advantage of altitude, I gradually started closing on the enemy aircraft and drew up to within 500yd [457m] astern and was about to open fire when the enemy aircraft cut his throttle and crash landed in a plowed field! He hit the ground just as I fired so I continued firing until within 100yd [91m] of him, observing many strikes around the cockpit and jet units. It skidded over several fields and came to a stop and caught fire. The pilot hopped out and started to run. The rest of my flight came over and strafed the plane and my #4 man [Lt. Croy] hit the pilot running away from the plane. The aircraft was burning brightly, giving off great clouds of black smoke. There were no propellers on the plane or on the ground near it."

It would be six weeks before another jet was encountered over the continent. Again, the 82nd Fighter Squadron was in the right place at the right time. Maj. Richard Conner shot down the first of two Me 262s credited to the 82nd Fighter Squadron in October. "After rendezvousing with the bombers, I took my section south and west of Hannover to

Left: With the introduction of the Me 262 to the skies above Europe the 8th and 9th Air Forces quickly issued this recognition handout.

Below: The Me 262 seen through Maj. Myers' gun camera, seconds before it hit the ground and skidded.

investigate a report of bandits in that area. While flying at 24,000ft [7,315m] in the immediate vicinity of several boxes of bombers with P-51 escort, I spotted two aircraft at about 12,000 to 14,000ft [3,658 to 4,267m], which I could not identify. I attempted to bounce using full power. Even with my altitude advantage, these aircraft outran me. I realized they were jet planes. Evidently short of fuel, they went to and started circling an airdrome north of Osnabruck. I attacked one and he outran me, then turned back toward me. His tactics seemed to be to fly away from me and attempt to turn back for a head-on pass.

"I was able to turn inside this aircraft and got several strikes on a 90-degree deflection shot. I got in another burst but missed. The enemy aircraft headed for the airdrome and I headed for him at full power. Suddenly he slowed and put down his wheels. I got one dead-astern shot, getting strikes, and then overran him and took evasive action from

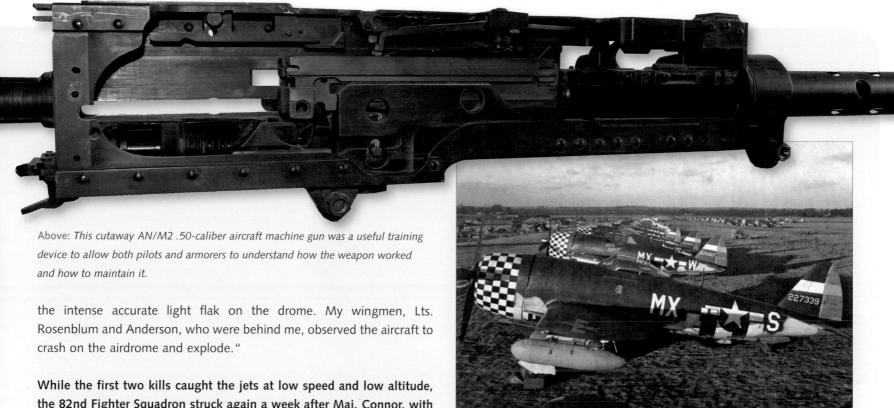

Above: *This cutaway AN/M2 .50-caliber aircraft machine gun was a useful training device to allow both pilots and armorers to understand how the weapon worked and how to maintain it.*

the intense accurate light flak on the drome. My wingmen, Lts. Rosenblum and Anderson, who were behind me, observed the aircraft to crash on the airdrome and explode."

While the first two kills caught the jets at low speed and low altitude, the 82nd Fighter Squadron struck again a week after Maj. Connor, with

Above: *Maj. Myers' personal Thunderbolt, P-47D-27-RE 42-27339, in which he claimed the Me 262 described in this section.*

Left: *Lt. Manford Croy (left) was given half credit for the destruction of the Me 262 jet during the action of August 28, 1944. Unfortunately, Croy was killed in action on April 16, 1945.*

Lt. Huie Lamb bouncing an Me 262 below him and finding that the Thunderbolt could easily turn inside the faster Messerschmitt and get a clear shot.

"Capt. Brown and I were returning from the Hannover area after strafing ground targets. Near Osnabruck, I spotted a jet aircraft at about

4,000ft [1,219m]. We were at about 15,000ft [4,571m] at this time. I started a steep dive and was indicating about 475 IAS and closing very fast. When I had closed to about 1,000yd [914m], he must have seen me, as he started to pick up speed and pulled away a little. I gave my plane full power and water and started to close on him again, but very slowly. As I got within range and started shooting, he started a turn to the left. I easily turned inside of him and kept shooting during the entire turn, noting many strikes. The enemy aircraft, an Me 262, made about a 180-degree turn and then leveled out. He started back and led me over an airfield that had been shooting flak at me as I chased the jet. I saw the intense curtain of flak coming up at me, but I followed him and got right on his tail, almost dead astern and noticed more strikes. He made another turn to the left and I kept firing and getting strikes. I felt myself being hit several times, but opened fire on him again from dead astern and noticed more strikes. He threw off his canopy and then the plane caught fire. The aircraft flipped over on its back and exploded. The flaming wreckage crashed into the ground and again exploded."

One Day, Three Jets

The 324th Fighter Group converted to the P-47 in the early summer 1944 and was one of the key groups that flew in support of the invasion of southern France. From then through the end of the war, the 324th flew in support of Seventh Army as it advanced through the sector. By April 1945, the group was flying from airfields in Alsace, striking airfields and rail networks deep within Germany.

The group's 316th Fighter Squadron flew several missions on April 4 and claimed jets destroyed on two of them. Lt. Mort "Tommy" Thompson led the early mission that day. "I was leading a twelve-ship formation of P-47s on an armed recce mission. Just south of Augsburg, Germany, I sighted an Ar 234 traveling west at 10,000ft [3,048m] at 0900hrs. I was flying at 13,000ft [3,962m] and I called a right turn and headed south and at the same time, the Ar 234 turned north. At that time I lost sight of him due to a cloud layer. A few seconds later, he appeared from beneath the clouds at the approximate position of 1 o'clock low. We dropped our bombs at 2,500ft [762m] and dove at 480mph [772kmh]. I immediately made a right diving turn upon him. I couldn't really see because the belly of the P-47 was too big, so had to guess where he'd be. When I leveled off, I was about 100yd [91m] behind him and I let him have it with the eight .50s. He bailed out

Left: Lt. Jerry Wurmser was flying number four in the top cover flight when he witnessed "Tommy" Thompson's Ar 234 kill on April 4. 1945.

Below: Lt. John Haun was the only pilot in the 324th Fighter Group to score two confirmed kills with head-on passes against enemy airplanes, one being the Me 262 he got on April 4, 1945.

immediately. I fired a two-second burst at close range and saw strikes enter approximately the middle of the fuselage. White smoke was seen to stream from his left nacelle. The Ar 234 then exploded, the pilot bailed out and the aircraft crashed. The German pilot thought he would be shot at, because that was what they had been instructed to do, but as I flew past, I saluted him and he saluted back."

Capt. J.T. Johnson was leading the second element in Thompson's lead flight and captured the critical gun camera footage of the Arado as it went down, confirming Thompson's kill: "As we watched, we surmised it was a jet job because of its speed. It seemed to turn in our direction (probably did not see us) and start a slight descent. I lost him in the haze but Thompson, my element leader, yelled, 'He's coming under us!' I said,

'Take him.' Tommy rolled under me and I rolled almost inverted; there it was, a twin-engined jet but not an Me 262. Anyway, Tommy pulled in behind him, started firing, and the ship started to burn. Tommy then pulled up and I followed in with more firing. Two people bailed out and the ship began to break up. It was almost like an unreal movie to see those two pilots pop right out in front of me. I was still firing and I wonder if I had hit either of them. As I broke off the pass, I could see that both chutes opened.

"Thompson had obviously made the kill because the ship was burning as I began firing, but it was a good thing I followed through. His gun camera had not worked, so he got credit for the kill but I got the pictures that proved it. We didn't know what we had shot down until we got back to base and dug through the picture books—an Arado 234 or 235 as I recall."

That afternoon, an eight-ship formation led by Lt. Andy Kandis was returning to base after a dive-bombing mission and were caught by a flight of Me 262s. Lt. John Haun, leading the second flight in Kandis' formation was the first to engage: "I was leading Blue Section of an eight-ship formation of P-47s on a dive-bombing mission. En route to base, after bombing and strafing, four Me 262s attacked our flight at about 9,000ft [2,743m] from out of the sun. We immediately turned into the attack and they broke off. They pulled up and continued making passes on us, but would not close in as long as we met them head-on. As one started to attack my section from behind, I turned into him again and started firing head-on. He stated to pull up and I pulled up with him and kept increasing my lead and firing long bursts as we closed. At the top of the pass, he fell

Below: *The G-3 and G-3A anti-G suits were introduced in late 1944. The garment was intended to keep pilots from passing out while executing high-G maneuvers.*

Above: *Mud was a huge problem in the spring of 1945 and hampered movement on the airfield at Lunéville, France.*

off to the left and started down in a steep dive with heavy smoke pouring out of the fuselage. I attempted to follow him down, but could not, as he went into the clouds at about 5,000ft [1,523m], still smoking badly."

Haun's Messerschmitt was later confirmed as destroyed, bringing his personal score to two confirmed kills, both shot down in head-on passes. Lt. Andy Kandis saw the 262 go in. After refueling and rearming Kandis went out on yet another mission, bagging a third jet for the day. "On a second mission that afternoon, I saw the jet taking off. I had altitude on him and was able to dive down on him. As I leveled out of the dive, I almost got in front him I was moving so fast. I ended up flying formation with him, although I didn't mean to. I look over at him, and he at me, and I could see his eyes bug out when he saw me on his wing. I dropped flaps, got in behind him and got a hold of him. One long burst and I had him. The plane exploded and the pilot did not make it out."

Lt. Ryland Dewey, Kandis' second element leader, caught another 262 and damaged it, but it got away. "My flight leader observed an enemy aircraft taking off from an airdrome near Munningen, Germany, and took lead section down on the enemy aircraft. As we were going down, I observed an Me 262 coming in at 9 o'clock so I made a pass at him, firing a long burst from 90 degrees and he flew through my fire. I then closed to a dead astern shot and observed strikes on the fuselage and pieces coming off the right side, the Me then did a wing over and started down. I thought he was going in, so I broke off, as we were only at about 500ft [152m]. The Messerschmitt then leveled off and was last seen on the deck, heading north."

Orange Tails Get in on the Game

While the 358th Fighter Group only brought down one confirmed jet, its 365th Fighter Squadron encountered a number of jets, damaging several. By April 17, 1945, the 365th was primarily operating over the Seventh Army sector in southern Germany. The squadron flew several missions throughout the day, encountering Me 262s on two of them. The first jets engaged Gatepost White Flight while escorting B-26s in the mid afternoon, and later Gatepost Red Flight was jumped by a lone jet while strafing ground positions.

Frederick Bishop was leading the second element in White Flight at around 1400hrs. "I was flying Gatepost White 3 escorting B-26s when an Me 262 made a stern attack on the #2 man. When the #2 broke, the enemy aircraft broke in front of me. I fired a deflection shot at him and followed through until it was a stern shot. I saw several strikes on the tail end but he just kept going. With a burst of speed, he pulled away from me and I turned back to the bombers. I saw another Me 262 but he was already engaged. He too broke and pulled away. We then re-formed and followed the bombers out."

Right: Ground crew personnel conduct maintenance on 365th Fighter Squadron Lt. Orin Wahl's "Helen Jo," P-47D-28-RA 42-29259. The ground grew had to work around the clock on hard-pressed P-47s to ensure their airworthiness.

were about to make their bomb run when I heard machine-gun fire and broke left and down. The enemy aircraft broke right and the rest of the flight went after him. I held my altitude and circled to clear myself. At this time I saw an Me 262 diving on a P-47. He was coming down at about a 30-degree to head on

Above: CP-X of the 367th Fighter Squadron, 358th Fighter Group, crash-landed near the 12th Armored Division's positions in April 1945.

Everett Heald, flying Red Leader's wing, also filed a "damaged" claim on another 262: "I was flying Gatepost White 2. White Leader had me standing by on C channel while the rest were on A channel. The bombers

Above: Another 367th Fighter Squadron Thunderbolt, CP- J, named "That's Urass," on an armed reconnaissance mission in the spring of 1945.

pass, so I put my sight well ahead of his line of flight and started firing. He rolled slightly just before the bullets hit, thus giving a plan view. I observed strikes on the underside of the fuselage and there was a small explosion on his right jet. He straightened out and flew straight away from me so I gave him another burst but saw no hits. When I last saw him he turned on his jet but only the left one was working."

Later that afternoon, Thomas Atkins jr. claimed one more Me 262 probably destroyed, but was unable to confirm the jet's destruction. "Gatepost Red Flight was in the process of strafing troop and gun positions in the northeastern section of Nurnberg. Yellow Flight was top cover at 8,000ft [2,438m]. I was Yellow Four. Red Two called over the radio that a jet was bouncing their flight. I looked down and saw the plane breaking over Red Leader, gradually turning south. I dove from 6,000ft [1,828m] with water injection and closed to about 1,000ft [305m]. I fired four long bursts, one after another. I saw strikes on his tail. At this moment, his plane shuddered, banking left and then right. I continued firing at him until he was out of range, still heading south into the haze. I broke off and White Leader observed an explosion in that direction. I was chasing him at an altitude of 1,000ft [305m] as he remained on the deck."

Above: The remains of the waterproofing window decal scraped off of a 365th Fighter Squadron CCKW 2.5-ton truck. The truck was fitted with its proper waterproofing in May 1944.

German Jets

While Germany's jet aircraft were too few and too late to have a significant impact on the war's outcome, they were cause for considerable concern for any Allied airmen who encountered them. The Luftwaffe had numerous designs on the drawing board, but only fielded three operational jet types in any significant numbers. The Messerschmitt Me 262A-1a *Schwalbe* (Swallow) was the most numerous, with more than 1,000 produced from 1943 to 1945. Its advanced aerodynamics, including a swept-back wing, gave it a top speed of more than

Right: *Camouflaged along the side of the road, this Me 262 fell victim to strafing P-47s in the closing weeks of the war, by which time the Luftwaffe had lost control of the airspace.*

540mph (869kmh], and 30mm cannon and R4M air-to-air rockets made it the ideal bomber-destroying interceptor. Yet the Me 262 suffered from several weaknesses, including an enormous turning radius that allowed Allied fighters to turn inside it, and temperamental engines that were often the pilot's worst enemy.

While not as numerous, the Ar 234 was still an important aeronautical achievement, as it was the world's first series-produced jet bomber. There were only 210 Ar 234 jets built, which were primarily used in the reconnaissance and bomber roles by Kampfgeschwader (bomber wing) 76 and a few smaller units, beginning in December 1944. Most notably, Ar 234B-2 bombers were used to attack the Ludendorff Bridge over the Rhine River at Remagen, Germany in March 1945. The straight-winged 234 was less of a technological marvel than the Me 262, with a top speed only slightly less than that of the P-47M but with significantly lower maneuverability.

Last to see series production was the Heinkel He 162 "Volksjager" or "People's Fighter," which was intended as a cheap, easy-to-produce single-engine jet interceptor. By April 1945, Jagdgeschwader (Fighter Wing) 1 had transitioned to the new fighter and had begun flying combat missions from Leck late in the month. The 162 was a rather advanced design with significant development potential, but suffered from quality-control issues in production that resulted in a number of in-flight structural failures during combat. As a result, JG1 only flew a handful of combat missions before the cessation of hostilities.

The POW Experience

"While there were German doctors in the hospital, none of them examined or treated me. I was treated by a Russian prisoner who had attended, but not finished, medical school. He took the plug out of my leg. One of the American Medical Corps men who were prisoners there treated my burns."

—Lt. Vincent Bower, 492nd Fighter Squadron

Capture was something that all pilots feared, but bailing out of a burning airplane was a far better course of action than the alternative. P-47 pilot Lt. Vincent Bower of the 492nd Fighter Squadron "hit the silk" after being hit while escorting his wingman's stricken airplane back to safety.

"On February 22, 1945, while on a mission escorting B-26s and dive-bombing near Siegen, my wingman's prop went out and he was losing altitude, so I started to escort him home. As we approached our lines, he was down to about 1,000ft [305m] and an easy target for flak, so I was strafing ahead of him to try to silence the flak guns; and in so doing, was hit myself. My aircraft started to burn and I was forced to bail out in the vicinity of Muleadu at about 1500hrs.

"I had the plug from a 20mm shell in my left leg below the knee and had first-degree burns on my face. I landed about 200yd [183m] from a barn and a civilian came running over with a gun pointed at me, apparently trying to make up his mind whether to shoot me, when German troops arrived and took me prisoner. They walked me into town, where I was given a cup of cold tea, and then they took me to a pillbox outside the town where a lieutenant and a major had me empty my pockets, taking and keeping my watch, my cigarette lighter, about 10,000 Belgian Francs, my jack knife, my driver's license, my AGO card, and my physical fitness card. They let me keep my wallet with pictures of my wife. There was an interrogator there who spoke very good English. He asked me my name, rank, and serial number, which I gave him. One of the items in my wallet was a newspaper clipping with my wife's picture, giving her address. The interrogator asked me for her address and when I told him I could not give him that information, he said he had it on the clipping, so it made no difference. He seemed to be very much interested in the whereabouts of my escape kit, maps, course data, etc. Actually I had not taken my escape kit with me, and the other things were burned in the aircraft, so I continued to tell him simply that I had none of those thing so could not surrender them to him. He seemed particularly interested in the escape kit and showed irritation over the fact that he could not get his hands on it. That was the extent of his interrogation and I was never again questioned.

"From the pillbox, we went on foot to Ginnick where I was given first aid and turned over to a guard whom I believe was an MP. We hitchhiked from there to Bonn to the Hangelar airfield, which we reached at about 0400hrs on February 23. I was permitted to sleep on a cot without blankets until shortly after daybreak, when a coal-burning truck took us to Siegburg. There I was put in a hospital and joined the inmates in time to partake of their noon meal of thin cabbage soup. Other than a small piece of Bologna which I had been given in Ginnick the previous afternoon, that was all the food I'd had until then.

"While there were German doctors in the hospital, none of them examined or treated me. I was treated by a Russian prisoner who had attended, but not finished, medical school. He took the plug out of my leg. One of the American Medical Corps men who were prisoners there treated my burns.

"I stayed at the hospital from February 23 until about March 18. The food was very inadequate. For breakfast we were given two pieces of black bread each and a cup of barley coffee. The supper menu was the same, while at noon the usual fare was a thin soup, either cabbage, sauerkraut, or bread soup. On Sundays the diet was implemented [sic] by potatoes, sliced beets, and a small piece of blood sausage. While I was a prisoner, I lost at least twenty pounds and I am convinced that many prisoners of all nationalities died of malnutrition. Shortly before I got there, twenty American prisoners had arrived from a Labor Battalion and about eight died, to my mind, from lack of food."

Right: Prisoners at the various POW camps for Army Air Forces personnel lived in relatively primitive conditions. Red cross packages like the one in the foreground were few and far between.

Last Licks

By the end of April 1945, it was clear the war was at an end. German forces were collapsing back into Germany at an increasing pace, the Russians were already in Berlin, and the US and Russian armies were meeting at Torgau on the Elbe River as combat in the skies overhead continued.

The 27th Fighter Group had fought from Sicily on through Italy and up through southern France. Initially equipped with A-36 dive-bombers, they begrudgingly converted to the P-47 in the summer of 1944. As part of XII TAC, they were primarily a ground-attack and close air support unit, but occasionally were tasked with escorting B-26s of the 9th Bomb Division. On April 24, 1945, the group's 524th Fighter Squadron encountered several Me 262s from Gen. Adolf Galland's Jagdverband 44 (JV44), damaging two. Two days later, the 524th finally was able to claim one, the final Messerschmitt jet of the war to be destroyed in air-to-air combat.

Above: Thunderbolt "S" of the 27th Fighter Group's 524th Fighter Squadron was flown by Lt. Irwin Lebow on the 12th Air Force's 500,000 fighter-bomber sortie.
Right: The Waltham A-11 pilot's watch was an essential piece of flight gear for operations, giving pilots an accurate timepiece to fly time-distance-heading to their targets.

Lt. John Lipiarz led the 524th's Blue Flight, escorting a vanguard of three B-26s ahead of the main formation: "Just before the B-26s made their bombing run, I was sent out with my flight to escort three B-26s dropping 'Window' [radar-confusing metal particles]. They flew at about 1,200ft [366m], doing evasive action and slighty ahead of the bomber formation. After the run was over, the three B-26s were maneuvering back into position with the rest of their formation, which was flying 270 degrees at the time. Just as the three bombers were at 9 o'clock and slightly low to the formation, Me 262s were called out making a pass from 5 or 6 o'clock. At the time, my wingman and I were at 3 o'clock to the three bombers while Blue 3 and 4 were at 9 o'clock. I first saw the two Me 262s when they were about 7 o'clock to me, closing at approximately 300mph [482kmh] and firing at the bombers. Before I could break more than 30 degrees, he went by me and through the formation of the three bombers, one of which was hit, and I started after him, flying through the debris. He started a steep left bank and went into a shallow dive accelerating quite rapidly. As he started to break, I already had a lead on him and I fired a short burst at 90 degrees and approximately 300yd [274m], which over-led him. I kept in this turn, turning inside him and decreasing the lead. I opened fire again at 60 degrees and 350yd [320m], firing in bursts, closing down to 0 degrees deflection and noticing strikes on the fuselage.

"Until I got to about 30 degrees, and turning inside, cutting him off, I stayed within 350yd [320m] of the enemy aircraft, but after that, he started pulling away. I fired until the enemy aircraft was approximately 500–600yd [away] and heading south. I broke off at this point and rejoined the bombers."

Lt. Jacob Ryseff, flying as Blue Two on Lt. Lipiarz's wing, confirmed the action: "I was flying Lt. Lipiarz's wing when two Me 262s attacked the B-26s we were escorting. The Me 262s came in at 6 o'clock to the bombers and about 7 o'clock to us. Lt. Lipiarz and I broke into the Me 262s just before they fired, but were unable to stop the attack. As the Me 262 fired and flew through the bomber formation, Lt. Lipiarz was able to fire on one of the Me 262s. I was not in position to fire, but I observed tracers from Lt. Lipiarz's guns striking the Me 262. There was not any visible damage to the Me 262, but I am sure that Lt. Lipiarz got hits on it. We were unable to continue the chase because the Me 262s were turning away from the bombers we were escorting."

Lt. Robert Prater also singled out a jet and like his flight leader, scored hits on it before the Messerschmitt broke off and escaped. "Just before the B-26s made their bombing run, Blue Flight, in which I was an element leader, was sent to escort three B-26s dropping 'window.' They flew at about 1,200ft [366m] doing evasive action and slightly ahead of the bomber

Left: The Flak 103/38 "Jaboschreck" mounted the 30mm MK103 cannon on a modified Flak 38 chassis, greatly improving the effectiveness of German AAA fire.

to me. I started to break into the first one, but he was almost past me by the time he was at 90 degrees. I gave him a short burst anyway and then concentrated on the second Me 262 which was about 300yd [274m] behind the first one. He started a turn and I turned with him and started firing at about 40 degrees and 400yd [366m]. I noticed the tracers going behind the tail but as the deflection angle closed down to 0 degrees, I could see strikes on the aircraft. I also made another pass head on to the same Me 262 but no results were observed."

Two days later, the 524th again tangled with an Me 262 from JV44 near Munich. Unlike the previous engagement, this was at low altitude and Capt. Herbert Philo caught the jet before it was able to accelerate away.
"I was leading White Flight in a strafing attack on a locomotive at Y-5454 when I saw an Me 262 heading east in front of me about 1 mile

Above: 523rd Fighter Squadron Thunderbolt named "Candie Jr" took a hefty 37mm antiaircraft hit in the left wing root during a dive-bombing mission in the spring of 1945. The image clearly shows the power of just one round.

Above: The 27th Fighter Bomber Group entered combat in 1943 as one of only three groups flying the A-36A Apache, the dive-bomber version of the Allison-engined P-51. The group transitioned to the P-40F and then the Thunderbolt in 1944.

formation. After the run was over, the three B-26s were maneuvering back into position with the rest of the bombers. Just as the three bombers were at 9 o'clock and slightly low to the formation, Me 262s were called out making a pass from 6 o'clock. At the time, my wingman and I were at 9 o'clock to the three bombers while Blue Leader and his wingman were at 3 o'clock. I first saw the Me 262s when they were about 5 o'clock

[1.6km] away. I chased the Me 262 about 13 miles [21km] and closed in to about 300yd [274m]. I opened fire but saw no hits.
"I continued to close to 100yd [91m]. I fired again and pieces began to break off the enemy aircraft. I pulled up to the left as the Me 262 started to fall off to the right. He hit the ground and exploded, the pilot did not get out."

Improving the Breed

"The leading Oscar had made a slow turn to the left as if to see what was going on behind when he saw me. I was closing in on him and he began a tight turn. . . . I had the advantage in that I was still out of firing range and had my throttle all the way back so that I could stay inside of his turn. . . . I caught him in my fixed crosshairs and led him as much as I could, firing all the way in."

—2nd Lt. Oscar Perdomo, 464th Fighter Squadron, August 13, 1945

The introduction of the new P-47N to the Central Pacific Theater of Operations was a game-changer. While the P-51D had begun flying Very Long Range (VLR) missions from Iwo Jima in April 1945, the Mustang simply could not carry the combat load that the Thunderbolt could bring to bear on the Japanese home islands. A flight of four P-47Ns carried a heavier bomb load and more .50-caliber machine guns than a pair of B-17s. They did it with sixteen fewer crewmen, at twice the airspeed, and, with the increased internal fuel of the N model, at an even greater range.

Four fighter groups took the P-47N into combat, three flying from the coral airstrips on Ie Shima, roughly 400 miles (644km) south of Kyushu. The 318th arrived on Ie Shima in the third week in May and immediately began preparations for combat. They were followed by the 413th Fighter Group in mid-June and the 507th Fighter Group in early July, bringing the 301st Fighter Wing up to full strength. The fourth group, the 414th, arrived on Iwo Jima in late June 1945 and launched a number of combat missions over northern Kyushu and southern Honshu before the cessation of hostilities.

Left: *The crew of an M2 halftrack looks on as a squadron of P-47N Thunderbolts return to Ie Shima after a combat mission over the Japanese home islands.*

The 318th Fighter Group was the first to re-equip with N models, in April 1945, and flew their first missions from Saipan to Truk lagoon in order to gain familiarity with the airplane's performance under combat conditions. These early missions, while considered "milk runs," were still quite dangerous. It was on one of these early missions that Lt. Earl Harbour of the 73rd Fighter Squadron scored the group's first kill in the new Thunderbolt: "My flight entered the Truk Lagoon at 1,200ft [366m] on a 180-degree course and spotted a bogey at 2 o'clock low at approximately 10 miles [16km]. [The] bogey was chased southeast for approximately 20 miles [32km] before catching him. I identified the bogey as an [Kawanishi H8K] Emily and made a slight deflection shot, falling back directly behind the plane.

"My fire was concentrated into the left inboard engine, wing root, and left side of the fuselage. I observed several pieces falling off and a fire was started in the engine. As I broke to the right, I saw one man got out of the right side of the cockpit and fall into the propeller. Another fell free from the midsection. The Emily, which swerved out of control, started to climb, stalled, and dove into the water. The plane burned and no survivors were seen." The 301st Fighter Wing would go on to score an impressive 161 kills over the Ryukyus and the Japanese home islands in the closing weeks of World War II.

Heckler Missions

The presence of American fighters over Japanese airfields was a shock to the Japanese military. Although B-29s had been hitting Japan for nearly a year, fighter escort from Saipan and Tinian was impossible due to the immense distances flown. Suddenly in April 1945, USAAF fighters taking off from US bases on Iwo Jima were able to fly the 700 miles [1,127km] to Japan, navigate to specific targets, strafe and bomb, and make the return trip to a small island in the Pacific. The 318th's arrival on Ie Shima narrowed that gap to 400 miles [644km] and greatly increased the radius of action over which American

fighters could operate over Japan. "Heckler" missions were intended specifically to target Japanese airfields and destroy the Japanese army and naval air forces, thereby allowing B-29 formations to operate with impunity over Japan. On May 28, the 19th Fighter Squadron launched twelve P-47Ns at 0816hrs, intending to strafe the airfields at Kanoya and Kushira. Lt. Lewis and F/O Hunter were forced to abort due to mechanical trouble. Cruising northeast at 13,000ft (3,962m), the remaining ten airplanes crossed the Japanese coast at 0930hrs, heading east toward the two airfields.

"Nine Zekes were observed taking off from East Kanoya airfield. They took off toward the east and turned north and headed up a valley." Maj. De Jack Williams jettisoned his tanks and started down from 11,000ft (3,353m). Five of the enemy planes were in three-ship and two-ship formations. Lining up the lead Zeke in his sights and screaming earthward at over 400mph [644km], Williams fired, seeing strikes on the wings and fuselage, but overshooting before he could see the Zeke crash.

Maj. Williams called for the flights to re-form at 15,000ft (4,572m) and as they did, four to five Zekes were called out at the same altitude. Williams' flight gave chase while Capt. Bill Loflin took his flight up to 20,000ft (6,096m) to provide top cover while Williams, Jackson, Sitton, and Thurston were giving Kanoya East airfield a thorough strafing.

While Maj. Williams opened up on the first Zeke, Capt. Loflin's flight continued to climb up to 20,000ft (6,096m) when they picked up five Zekes headed towards them. Thunderbolts and Zekes dropped their external fuel tanks almost simultaneously and the Japanese pilots aggressively turned toward the P-47s. Four Zekes attacked Capt. Loflin,

Top, left and right: Captain John Vogt (left) and Lt. Stanley Lustic (right) became the second and third pilots to "make ace" in the P-47N.

Above: Although the 318th began operations from Ie Shima in May 1945, the airfield was not yet complete. The runway was too short for a fully loaded P-47N to take off safely and a number of crashes occurred before the runway was lengthened.

and Lt. Lustic came to his aid, immediately chasing two off and getting solid hits on a third, which flamed and crashed.

The second Zeke attacked, then split-S'd away with Lustic's "Stanley's Steamer" (P-47N 44-87858) closing quickly behind. Lustic adjusted his gunsight and fired at roughly 3,000ft [914m], where the Zeke flamed and went straight in. Stan Lustic had just scored kills five and six, making him the 318th's second ace in less than a week.

An hour after Stan Lustic landed as the group's second ace in a week, Capt. John Vogt was taking off in his P-47N "Drink'n Sister" (44-87911), on another Heckler mission to keep the pressure on Kanoya airfield. Only seven of the twelve Thunderbolts launched continued the mission. As they reached Kyushu and reconnoitered the airfields at 15,000ft [4,572m], the flight spotted a formation of twenty-eight Zekes inbound at 19,000ft [5,791m]. The Japanese formation had at least a handful of experienced pilots and tried to execute a Lufberry circle once the P-47s were spotted climbing up to meet them.

"We retained our external fuel tanks and climbed to 21,000ft [6,400m] at 1,000ft [305m] a minute, pulling 50in [127cm] of mercury. The Zekes also started to climb. We dropped our tanks upon reaching 21,000ft [6,400m] and continued to climb west using full War Emergency Power until we reached 28,000ft [8,534m], giving us a 1,000ft [305m] altitude advantage over the enemy." Realizing the Americans were above them, the Japanese quickly dispersed, diving in all directions just as Capt. Vogt and his wingman, Lt. La Rochelle, attacked. Vogt's first victim caught a 30-degree deflection shot right at the wing root and the Zeke exploded.

Still in a shallow dive, Vogt immediately got on the tail of another Zeke and sent it down in flames. The two Americans then pulled in behind a Japanese two-ship element with a third in trail. Lt. La Rochelle knocked down the straggler quickly, while Vogt opened fire, first on the wingman and then on the Japanese flight leader.

The Japanese pilots they encountered were far more experienced and aggressive than any that had been encountered previously. Another Zeke

attempted to pull up into Capt. Vogt, but he fired on the Zeke as it stalled trying to maintain position. Vogt's .50-caliber rounds went directly into the canopy and fuselage, obliterating it and confirming kill number four.

Another Zeke attempted to line up Vogt for a firing pass, but Vogt turned into the Zeke and they closed, head-on and firing. The Zeke continued to close, when finally Vogt's rounds found their mark and the Zeke exploded. The remaining Zekes fled in disarray as Vogt's Cossack 121 Flight turned to head home.

While the quality of Japanese pilots had diminished significantly, the May 28 fight clearly showed that Japan's aviators were not finished. However, it was evident that the once-invincible A6M Zeke, vaunted for its incredibly small turning radius, could not turn with the P-47N.

May 1945 had been an extremely successful month for the 318th Fighter Group, with fifty-five confirmed kills between the three squadrons (forty-one, seven, and seven respectively between the 19th, 73rd, and 333rd). As the war continued through the summer, the 318th would continue to have similar successes, to end the war as the top-scoring P-47N group.

Kamikaze Killers

The 1st Fighter Squadron had only just settled in to their new accommodations on Ie Shima when they began flying combat missions in late June 1945. The eager pilots did not have to wait long to hunt down enemy aircraft and start running up the squadron's score.

An early launch on June 22 had Capt. Robert Allard's flight lifting off at 0530hrs on a fighter sweep north of Okinawa. One of the eight airplanes, flown by Lt. Albert Macata, aborted just after takeoff and returned to base. The remaining seven airplanes continued to climb through the overcast on instruments, finally popping out of the murk at 7,000ft [2,134m]. They then turned toward enemy-held Amami-O Shima and descended through a hole in the clouds down to 400ft [122m]. Capt. George Fuller was forced to turn back at this point due to mechanical troubles.

The patrol route was designed to intercept any incoming Japanese aircraft headed for the anchorages either at Ie Shima or Okinawa. It took a northeasterly route along the west side of the Amami Island chain, to Takarajima, before turning southwest to return to Ie Shima along the

Above: *Capt. Frank Vetort flew the majority of his eighteen combat missions with the 413th Fighter Group in P-47N-2-RE 44-87971, named "Knocked Up."*

Above: *Two 21st Fighter Squadron ground crew members working in the hot Ie Shima sun on one of the squadron's new N-model Thunderbolts. The fighter's large K-14 gunsight is clearly visible through its windscreen.*

eastern coastline of the islands. Lt. Alfred Danielson, one of the three element leaders, relates: "We'd been circling the Amami group for about two hours and it was now 0800hrs and we were going through a pass at about 1,000ft [305m], rounding a lighthouse and heading home when there they were!"

Capt. Robert Allard, the mission commander, was shocked at seeing the perfect box formation of fourteen bomb-laden Ki-43 Oscars with blue tail stripes at about 500ft [152m], heading toward and under the Thunderbolts "I could have shit a brick! I looked down and there were fourteen of them! I wasn't sure at first, suppose they were our planes? So we started down—turning, diving, and staying in paths of twos. Then I could see they were Oscars. I got on the tail of one and scored hits on the right wing. I didn't see it go down, but Murphy did.

"When I got my second plane into position and started firing, I could see chunks of the airplane stuff flying off of the Jap plane. Then it began smoking and glided toward the water. It seemed to burst apart all at once and the explosion blinded me for a couple seconds. After that, I had a dogfight with one up to about 5,000ft [1,524m], but he got away. I was not able to get good bursts on him from the rear due to his evasive action, which consisted of making tight turns to the left and turning inside my turns. I maneuvered into a head-on pass and fired one burst."

Meanwhile, Lt. Dean Murphy, Allard's wingman, confirmed his lead's kill and then lined up an Oscar of his own. He fired at long range and then began to close the distance to improve his chances at an effective hit, but before he could fire, the Oscar peeled off and exploded when it hit the water. "I think I killed the pilot on the first burst."

The rest of the flight was working over the remaining enemy aircraft. Lts. Danielson and Haggerty pounced on a pair of stragglers. In their post-mission interview, both pilots agreed "We will never lag behind in formation because we nailed two stragglers right off the bat." Danielson's Oscar "turned to the left and then immediately reversed to the right. I kept on him, my first burst started biting big chunks off of him

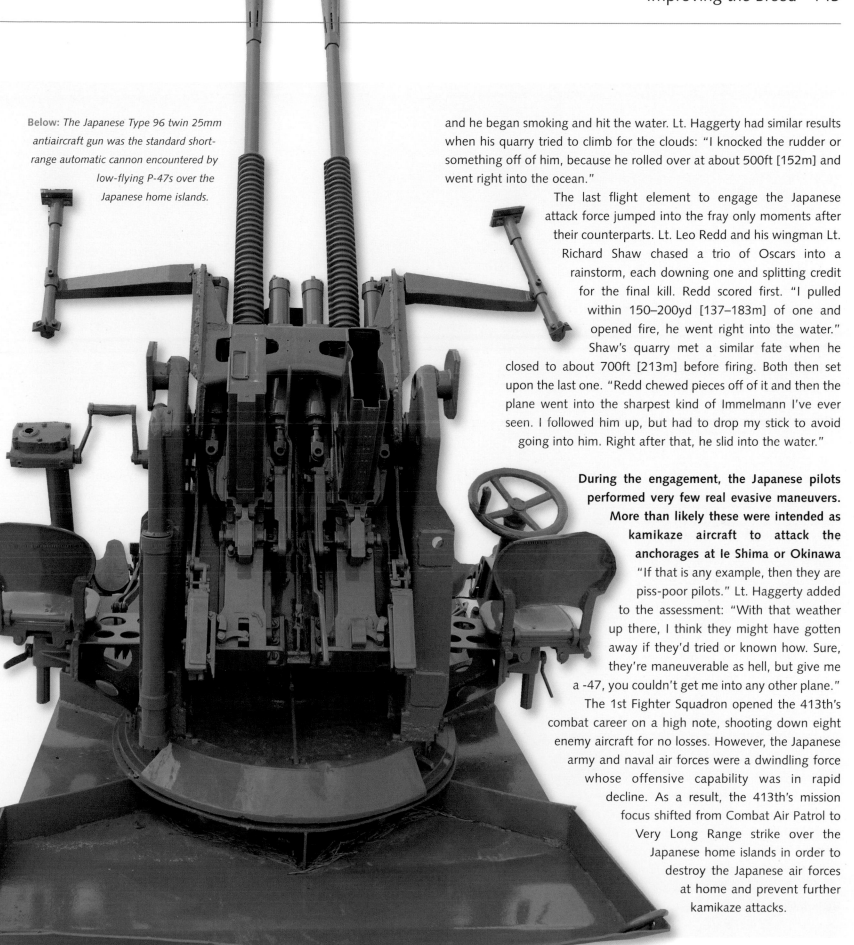

Below: *The Japanese Type 96 twin 25mm antiaircraft gun was the standard short-range automatic cannon encountered by low-flying P-47s over the Japanese home islands.*

and he began smoking and hit the water. Lt. Haggerty had similar results when his quarry tried to climb for the clouds: "I knocked the rudder or something off of him, because he rolled over at about 500ft [152m] and went right into the ocean."

The last flight element to engage the Japanese attack force jumped into the fray only moments after their counterparts. Lt. Leo Redd and his wingman Lt. Richard Shaw chased a trio of Oscars into a rainstorm, each downing one and splitting credit for the final kill. Redd scored first. "I pulled within 150–200yd [137–183m] of one and opened fire, he went right into the water." Shaw's quarry met a similar fate when he closed to about 700ft [213m] before firing. Both then set upon the last one. "Redd chewed pieces off of it and then the plane went into the sharpest kind of Immelmann I've ever seen. I followed him up, but had to drop my stick to avoid going into him. Right after that, he slid into the water."

During the engagement, the Japanese pilots performed very few real evasive maneuvers. More than likely these were intended as kamikaze aircraft to attack the anchorages at Ie Shima or Okinawa "If that is any example, then they are piss-poor pilots." Lt. Haggerty added to the assessment: "With that weather up there, I think they might have gotten away if they'd tried or known how. Sure, they're maneuverable as hell, but give me a -47, you couldn't get me into any other plane."

The 1st Fighter Squadron opened the 413th's combat career on a high note, shooting down eight enemy aircraft for no losses. However, the Japanese army and naval air forces were a dwindling force whose offensive capability was in rapid decline. As a result, the 413th's mission focus shifted from Combat Air Patrol to Very Long Range strike over the Japanese home islands in order to destroy the Japanese air forces at home and prevent further kamikaze attacks.

VLR Escort

While the P-47N was the optimum Very Long Range (VLR) escort fighter, the 301st Fighter Wing only flew one B-29 escort mission. On August 8, 1945, 140 Thunderbolts from all three Ie Shima-based groups took off at 0745hrs to rendezvous with 221 B-29s of the 73rd Bomb Wing 21,000ft [6,400m] over Novoritate.

Left: Propaganda leaflet dropped by US aircraft over Japan warning of continued B-29 bombing raids unless Japan surrenders.

At 1020hrs, 1st Lt. Jack Sanford's flight of the 1st Fighter Squadron was escorting the lead bomber elements at 20,000ft [6,095m] en route to Yawata. "I saw at least two enemy aircraft at 17,000ft [5,181m] parallel to the bomber formation and going in the opposite direction. The enemy planes were to the right of the bombers and below. We were further to the right and above. Taking my wingman Lt. Hollis, we peeled off and went in to attack. I came in at 7 o'clock to the enemy and waited until I saw the red meatballs on his ship, which was painted a dark green, before I opened fire. My first burst caught him in the right wing at a range of 300ft [91m]. My second burst hit his fuselage as he skidded toward the bomber formation. The enemy pilot bailed out and his plane was completely on fire and was seen to explode before hitting the ground."

Sanford's wingman, 2nd Lt. Edward Hollis, picked up the second Japanese airplane as his lead attacked the first. "Lt. Sanford took the first and I the second. I gave him a burst from 300ft [91m] into the left wing and as he skidded toward the bombers, smoke and flame broke out. I put another burst into him and he started to go down and was seen to completely explode before hitting the ground. Enemy pilots were not evasive or aggressive and seemed unaware of our attack. To the best of my knowledge the enemy plane was a Zeke 52 and was painted a dark green, almost black."

Meanwhile, fifty-three Thunderbolts of the 507th Fighter Group were the first to sight enemy aircraft as they passed Mumamoto. Capt. William Morris' flight of four from the 463rd Fighter Squadron was the first to engage the Japanese Air Force. "I was flying on the left top of the bomber formation when I saw a black or dark-colored [Kawasaki Ki-61] Tony flying above me. I pushed the throttle forward and started to climb up underneath him, climbing from 19,000ft [5,791m] to almost 21,000ft [6,400m]. He would turn up on his wing to see if anyone was underneath him, but apparently he did not see me until he was almost within range, when he saw me and started a tight turn to the left. I turned with him and gave him a burst. I saw bullets strike the cowling behind the engine, the windshield, and the left wing root just below the cockpit. When I hit him, he fell into a tight spiral down and then into a spin. It appeared that some of the shots had hit the cockpit."

Capt. Morris' flight quickly rejoined the bomber stream, while a second flight from the 463rd, led by Capt. John Kelly, swooped down on a twin-engined Kawasaki Ki-45 "Nick" bomber-destroyer. "We approached the target from the southwest. When it came time for us to pull away from the bombers as they started the bomb run, I knew we were to turn left to the rally point, but there was too much flak that way. I led my flight to the right and made a 270-degree turn. On our way to meet the bombers again, we crossed the northwest coast of Kyushu just north of Gannoshu, making a climbing turn to the left. At 1120hrs at 23,000ft [7,010m], I called out a Nick making a left turn to pass under us. My flight, consisting of Lts. Rodman, Wallick, and Rampy, was

Above: Cleaning the guns: .50-caliber machine guns were cleaned after every combat mission to ensure proper function in combat. Between carbon buildup and the ever-present coral dust on Ie Shima, this was no small task.

Left: *Capt. Randal Hathway's Thunderbolt burns fiercely after crashing on takeoff. Hathway was rescued in the nick of time by SSgt. James G. Love and Sgts. George Moore and David Pierson.*

fuselage just aft of the cockpit. The cockpit immediately filled with smoke and hydraulic fluid. I jettisoned the canopy, rolled the ship onto its back and attempted to fall free. When I released the stick, the airplane nosed down and pinned me in the cockpit for thirty to sixty seconds. When I finally got out, I fell about 5,000ft [1,524m] before opening my chute. I then lit a cigarette, took out my compass, and oriented myself. Within thirty minutes of hitting the water, a B-17 sighted me and dropped a lifeboat. The drop was very good and I reached and boarded the boat without difficulty." Four days later, he was picked up by a "Dumbo" PBY from the 6th Emergency Rescue Squadron.

The 301st Fighter Wing's sole escort mission resulted in thirteen confirmed kills for a loss of two P-47Ns due to flak. One B-29 was lost to enemy fighters during the bombing run and limped out to sea before ditching, while one more went down due to enemy antiaircraft fire.

stacked to the left. We made a diving left turn into him going into a string formation. We attacked from the rear making all tail shots. We all shot at him and pulled up to the right. I looked down and saw Rampy, the number four man, shoot off his right wing and right engine at about 17,000ft [5,181m]. The rest of the plane then practically fell apart in the air. The plane was a Nick apparently very new of a shiny OD color. No chutes were seen and there is no doubt that the plane was destroyed."

Antiaircraft fire over the target and along the ingress route was heavy-caliber, accurate, and moderate in intensity. The Japanese had begun using white phosphorous in their antiaircraft projectiles, inflicting at least one of the two P-47 losses from the 19th Fighter Squadron flown by F/O Jesse Hill. "I was hit by a burst of white phosphorous flak at about 1020hrs at an altitude between 25,000 and 27,000ft [7,620 and 8,230m] off the northern tip of Kyushu. Fragments struck the left wing in several places and started a fire in the

Below: Judging from the empty hardpoints and chocks still in place, "Dotty" from the 464th Fighter Squadron is about to launch either on a local Combat Air Patrol or on a maintenance test flight.

Nose Art

While artwork adorned just about every type of aircraft flown by the USAAF in World War II, the Thunderbolt was a particularly broad canvas that invited artwork of all kinds. Nose art artists ranged from ground crew members to pilots, and in many cases to a designated squadron artist who did all of the unit's artwork.

Nose art boosted morale. Whether depicting a Disney character, a buxom blonde or brunette, or something completely different, the artwork broke up the uniformity of military life and allowed for some personalization of the war. Talented and trained artists like Thunderbolt pilot George Rarey of the 379th Fighter Squadron were in demand to paint artwork not only on the squadron's airplanes, but on officers' club walls, squadron HQ, and just about any other flat surface possible.

This spread: Nose art was a reminder of home and a psychological escape from the insanity of war. Whether the artwork adorning a P-47 was a scantily clad female, the squadron's insignia, or simply a name, it was a method for pilots and ground crews to personalize their airplane. By doing so, the artwork infused the airplane with its own identity and character, making it a living, breathing being instead of simply a mindless machine of war.

The Great Korean Turkey Shoot

By August 13, 1945, both Hiroshima and Nagasaki had been reduced to radioactive ash and the Japanese high command was split between continuing the war and surrender. Yet that day would prove to be the 507th Fighter Groups's longest mission and one that would earn the unit a Distinguished Unit Citation. The 464th Fighter Squadron would claim fourteen of the seventeen enemy aircraft downed. Lt. Oscar Perdomo also became the last ace of World War II, earning the Distinguished Service Cross for his ace-in-a-day mission.

"Major Jarman dived on the closest Jap and I followed behind with my element. The number two Jap split-S'd and disappeared under the clouds, so I turned sharply to the right to go after the last three that had turned to the right but were still visible.

"I pushed the throttle into water injection with the prop pitch at about 2,700rpm. As I gained on the Oscars I placed my gyro sight on the last one and adjusted the sight diamonds on his wings. At this time the Oscars were flying a very loose vee. When I closed into firing range, I gave him a burst and saw my bullets converge on his nose and cockpit. Something exploded in his engine and fire broke out. I was still shooting as he fell to the right.

"I pulled away over to the Jap on my right when I saw my first Oscar explode in the air. I lined up immediately on this second ship and began firing at about 30 degrees. I shot at this Oscar until parts flew off and fire broke out on the bottom cowling of his engine. I ceased firing when he rolled over slowly and dove straight into the ground and exploded. At this time, I would have gone after the Jap flight leader if either of these two first Oscars were still in the air now behind me.

"The leading Oscar had made a slow turn to the left as if to see what was going on behind when he saw me. I was closing in on him and he began a tight turn. Still to the left, gaining speed, and streamers were trailing off his wingtips. I had the advantage in that I was still out of firing range and had my throttle all the way back so that I could stay inside of his turn. Streamers were pouring off my own wings beginning at the

Target Pattern Right and Wrong

Correct—You have exact range now. Fire!

Incorrect—Dot is not on target.

Correct—Circle of diamonds corresponds to target's wing span.

Incorrect—Circle of diamonds is too large, making range and lead angle wrong.

Correct—On broadside attacks the circle should be a trifle larger than length of fuselage, as wing span is greater than length.

Incorrect—Imaginary circle formed by inner tips of diamonds should correspond to target's wing span.

54

roots. I caught him in my fixed crosshairs and led him as much as I could, firing all the way in.

"He continued his spiral turn about 180-degrees until he was about 100ft [30m] off the ground. Then he hit a high-speed stall, because I saw his airplane shudder and it snapped him still tighter to the left and into the ground where he exploded like a napalm bomb.

Left: The "right and wrong" page in the pilot's manual was an attempt at making the process of using the stabilized, computing K14 gunsight much easier.

Below left: Lt. Oscar Perdomo is seen here with a Republic Aircraft Corporation technical representative. Below right: Lt. Oscar Perdomo in "Meatie's" cockpit shortly after the cessation of hostilities.

"I put my throttle forward and started back towards town. As I came back I could see the fires from my first Oscar and there above was a man in a parachute. I trained my sight on him until I closed in. He was a Jap in a leather flying suit or a shiny green one. I didn't press my trigger; instead I rocked my wings. I kept climbing up to 1,500ft [457m] looking for our P-47s.

"After a little bit, I saw two [Yokosuka K5Y] Willows flying in formation at about 800ft [244m]. I pulled back my throttle and went down after them. They saw me at the last minute and separated. I picked the closest to me and started shooting. Flame broke out almost immediately. To slow my ship up, I crossed my controls and skidded. Then I shot some more at him. This time I must have hit the pilot because the ship went into a spiral to the right and straight into the ground about 300ft [91m] below.

"I started climbing above the clouds when all of a sudden three or four Oscars broke out above me and to my right about 120 degrees. I turned into them and pointed my nose down, hoping they hadn't seen me, but we were too close to each other. I shot under them and poured water injection on and turned into the cloud.

"As I came in on these Oscars, three of them turned left and one turned right. I followed the single one and used my gyro sight. His only evasive maneuvers were turns. I shot at him in bursts until he flamed. He exploded when I pulled up alongside because of my excessive speed. The mass of flame went into the ground.

"Once more I headed back toward the city and the rest of our group. As I came over the airfield, I saw two P-47s shooting an Oscar, but the Oscar out-turned them, leaving himself wide open to me. I dived on his tail and began to shoot when I was right on him. He pulled streamers in his turn, but I managed to stay in, shooting all the time.

"Just when I could almost reach out and touch him, my guns quit. I hoped he didn't guess it and I flew right under him so that he couldn't see me. He turned one way and then another, finally racking it up to the left. I broke right and down, pouring on water injection. I saw a yellow-tailed P-47 out of the corner of my right eye and yelled at him to shoot the Oscar off my tail."

Perdomo's wingman, Lt. Harry Steinshouer, had remained stuck to his flight lead's wing throughout most of the engagement, and in a textbook example of lead-wing mutual support, Steinshouer found himself with a perfect shot to knock down the Oscar. "The Oscar started a turn to the left and my element leader broke right. The Oscar immediately made a sharp turn to the right and opened fire. I closed to 1,000ft [305m] and opened fire and the enemy plane started

Left: The K-14 gunsight. The pilot needed simply to dial in the approximate wingspan of his target and follow the diamonds on his illuminated reticle.

smoking. I fired at him all the way to the ground and he exploded. "

The 301st Fighter Wing continued flying combat missions over Japan on August 15, 1945, until the code word "UTAH" was broadcast that afternoon, signifying the Japanese had finally accepted surrender terms and ending the four-year conflict during which the P-47 was designed, developed, and became the ultimate American piston-engine fighter of World War II.

Above: Although Ie Shima was a relatively small island, it was overflowing with aircraft of all types. The 463rd Fighter Squadron dispersal area is visible here, with the 464th and 465th farther in the distance.

Further Reading

The 350th Fighter Group in the Mediterranean Campaign 2 November 1942 to 2 May 1945 (Schiffer 1997)

Bernstein, Jonathan. *P-47 Units of the Twelfth Air Force* (Osprey 2012)

Bodie, Warren. *Republic's P-47 Thunderbolt: From Seversky to Victory* (Widewing Publications, 1994)

Boehme, Manfred. JG7: *The World's First Jet Fighter Unit 1944–1945* (Schiffer, 1992)

Bowman, Martin. W. *Great American Air Battles of World War II* (Airlife 1994)

Bowman, Martin. W. *Four Miles High* (PSL, 1992)

Buchholtz, Chris. *332nd Fighter Group Tuskeegee Airmen* (Osprey, 2007)

Calling Jackpot: Story of the 66th Fighter Squadron (Italy, 1945)

Colgan, William B. *Allied Strafing in World War II: A Cockpit View of Air to Ground Battle* (McFarland & Co, 2001)

Cora, Paul B. *Yellowjackets! The 361st Fighter Group in World War II* (Schiffer, 2002)

Cross, G.E. *Jonah's Feel Are Dry: The Experiences of the 353rd Fighter Group During World War II* (Thunderbolt Publishing, 2001)

Dean, Francis H. *America's Hundred Thousand: US Production Fighters of World War Two* (Schiffer 1997)

Dodds, Wayne S. *The Fabulous Fifty Seventh Fighter Group of World War II* (Walsworth Publishing Co, 1985)

Duxford Diary 1942–1945 (W. Heffer & Sons, 1945)

The Falcon: 79th Fighter Group, USAAF (F. Bruckmann, 1946)

Freeman, *Roger. The Mighty Eighth* (Doubleday, 1970)

Freeman, Roger. *The Mighty Eighth War Manual* (Motorbooks International, 1984)

Fry, Garry L. and Ethell, Jeffrey L. *Escort to Berlin: the 4th Fighter Group in World War II* (Arco Publishing 1980)

Girbig, Werner. *Six Months to Oblivion* (Schiffer, 1991)

Gotts, Steve. *Little Friends: A Pictorial History of the 361st Fighter Group in World War II* (Taylor Publishing 1993)

Green, Herschel. *Herky: Memoirs of a Checkertail Ace* (Schiffer, 1996)

Groh, Richard. *The Dynamite Gang: The 367th Fighter Group in World War II* (Aero Publishers, 1983)

Hess, Bill. *Aces and Wingmen II* (Aviation Usk, 1999)

Hughes, Thomas Alexander. *Over Lord: General Pete Quesada and the Triumph of Tactical Air Power in World War II* (Free Press, 2002)

Luce, Steve W. *86th Fighter Group in World War II* (Eagle Editions, 2007)

McDowell, Ernest. *Checkertails: The 325th Fighter Group in the Second World War* (Squadron, 1994)

McDowell, Ernest. *Thunderbolt: The Republic P-47 Thunderbolt in the Pacific Theater* (Squadron, 1999)

McFarland, Stephen L. and Newton, Wesley Phillips. *To Command The Sky* (Smithsonian, 1991)

McLachlan, Ian. *USAAF Fighter Stories* (Haynes Publishing, 1997)

McLachlan, Ian. *USAAF Fighter Stories: A New Selection* (Sutton Publishing, 2005)

Miller, Kent. *The 365th Fighter Squadron in World War II* (Schiffer, 2006)

Mombeek, Eric. *Defending the Reich: The History of JG1 Oeseau* (JAC Publications, 1992)

Morris, Danny. *Aces and Wingmen I* (Aviation Usk, 1989)

O'Leary, Michael. *VIII Fighter Command at War: "Long Reach"* (Osprey Publishing, 2000)

Parker, Danny S. *To Win the Winter Sky* (Combined Books, 1994)

Patterson, Michael. *Battle for the Skies: From Europe to the Pacific* (David & Charles, 2004)

Pons, Gregory. *9th Air Force: American Tactical Aviation in the ETO 1942–1945* (Histoire et Collections, 2008)

Price, Alfred. *The Last Year of the Luftwaffe: May 1944 to May 1945* (Arms & Armour, 1991)

Rust, Kenn C. *The 9th Air Force in World War II* (Aero Publishers, 1967)

Scutts, Jerry. *P-47 Aces of the Eighth Air Force* (Osprey, 1998)

Scutts, Jerry. *P-47 Aces of the Ninth and Fifteenth Air Forces* (Osprey, 1999)

Speer, Frank E. *The Debden Warbirds: The 4th Fighter Group in World War II* (Schiffer, 1999)

Stanaway, John. *Kearby's Thunderbolts* (Schiffer, 1997)

Van Wagner, R. D. Any Place, *Any Time, Any Where: The 1st Air Commandos in World War II* (Schiffer, 1998)

Wells, Ken. *Steeple Morden Strafers 1943-1945* (East Anglian Books, 1994)

Woerpel, Don. *The 79th Fighter Group over Tunisia, Sicily and Italy in World War II* (Schiffer 2001)

Glossary

AAA Antiaircraft Artillery

ASR Air Sea Rescue

BG Bomb Group

Bogies Unidentified (probably hostile) aircraft

Bounce Attack on an enemy aircraft from an altitude advantage

Burst One brief press of the trigger

Cannon Weapon that fires explosive projectiles

CAVU Ceiling And Visibility Unlimited, i.e clear skies

CBI China-Burma-India Theater of Operations

Chandelle A climbing turn resulting in a 180-degree change in direction

Column cover Coordination between friendly armored units and overhead P-47s through a P-47 pilot assigned to a tank crew

Compressibility The separation of airflow over an airfoil due to the formation of transonic and supersonic shockwaves as an airplane's speed increases

Deflection The angle from which the shooting fighter attacks an adversary. Zero degrees deflection is directly behind the enemy aircraft, whereas 90 degrees would be a direct side attack. Computing the angle of deflection allows the pilot to estimate the necessary amount of lead to insure the rounds meet the target airplane at a predetermined point in space.

Dinah Japanese Army Air Force Ki-46 reconnaissance aircraft

Diver German V-1 cruise missile

Doodlebug German V-1 cruise missile

The Drink The sea (English Channel, Mediterranean, Pacific, etc)

Dumbo Air Sea Rescue airplane, usually an OA-10 Catalina amphibian, that can land directly on the water

E/A Enemy Aircraft

Eagle Squadrons American Volunteer squadrons in the Royal Air Force that eventually became the 4th Fighter Group

Escort fighter A fighter airplane designed to escort bomber formations to and from their target, deterring and also responding to enemy fighter attacks

ETO European Theater of Operations

Evansville The second Republic Aircraft factory at Evansville, Indiana

FAC Forward Air Controller

Farmingdale Republic Aircraft's original factory at Farmingdale, Long Island, New York

Fighter Group (FG) An Army Air Forces organization comprised of three fighter squadrons, a headquarters squadron, and a maintenance squadron.

Fighter Squadron (FS) The basic Army Air Forces fighter unit. The single-engine fighter squadron had twenty-five airplanes and 284 officers and men assigned.

Flak Abbreviation of *FlugzeugAbwehrKanone* (antiaircraft gun); the term was used by the Allies to refer to antiaircraft fire

Frank Japanese Army Air Force Ki-84 fighter plane that replaced the Ki-43 Oscar

GI Government Issue, a US serviceman

Gruppe A German fighter unit roughly the size of an American fighter group

HE High-explosive, usually in reference to bombs, rockets, or cannon ammunition

Heavies Friendly four-engine bombers

Horsefly A P-47 pilot forward air controller flying an L-5 Sentinel that directs fighter bombers onto various ground targets

HEI High-Explosive Incendiary—cannon ammunition designed to explode and start fires

HVAR High Velocity Aircraft Rocket

IAS Indicated Air Speed

IFF Identification Friend or Foe; the P-47's SCR-535 IFF transponder

IO Intelligence Officer

IP Initial Point—the beginning point for a bomb run

Jagdgeschwader German fighter wing, composed of three to four *Gruppen*

Jagdverband Fighter unit, e.g. Jagdverband 44, General Adolf Galland's elite Me 262 jet unit

Jagdwaffe German fighter force

Jug Short for Juggernaut, a P-47

KIA Killed in Action

Line Abreast A fighter formation where all airplanes are flying parallel courses and are spread directly out from the flight leader's wingtip in a straight line

Little Friend Fighter escorts for the bombers

Lufbery The Lufbery Circle was a defensive maneuver in which a group of aircraft fly in a tight circle, covering the tail of the aircraft in front of them. This made it difficult for attacking aircraft to target a single airplane without themselves being targeted by the following aircraft

Luftwaffe The German Air Force

Milk Run An easy mission

MTO Mediterranean Theater of Operations

Napalm A combination of naphthalic and palmitic acids to form a gelling agent along with gasoline. An incendiary bomb first experimented with in the MTO by 57th Fighter Group P-47s that eventually saw service in all theaters

NCO Non-commissioned officer; an enlisted soldier in the rank of Sergeant or higher

PoW Prisoner of War

Purple Heart Award given to soldiers who received wounds or were killed in combat.

PX Post Exchange

Oscar Japanese Army Air Force Ki-43 fighter

R&R Rest and Relaxation

R/T Radio Telephone

RCAF Royal Canadian Air Force

Recce An abbreviation for the word "Reconnaissance"

Rover Joe Ground-based forward air control element usually consisting of a P-47 pilot,

driver, and a radio-equipped jeep for guiding overhead fighter-bombers onto their targets

RP Rocket Projectile

Sack Bed

Sortie One mission flown by one aircraft

Split-S An air combat maneuver used to descend rapidly and change direction 180-degrees. The pilot rolls inverted and pulls downward, resulting in significant loss of altitude, higher speed, and complete reversal of direction

Supercharger Compresses the air supplied to an engine, giving each intake cycle of the engine more oxygen, letting it burn more fuel and do more work, thus increasing power.

Table of Organization and Equipment (TO&E) Table that denotes all personnel and equipment authorized for a military unit. The Army Air Forces Single Engine Fighter Squadron uses TO&E 1-27.

TAC Tactical Air Command

TALO Tactical Air Liaison Officer; an Army Air Forces Officer, usually a pilot, assigned to a ground unit to facilitate air-ground coordination

UHF Ultra High Frequency Radio; P-47's SCR-522A radio

USAAC United States Army Air Corps

USAAF United States Army Air Forces (after June 20, 1941)

USSTAF US Strategic and Tactical Air Forces

VHF Very High Frequency Radio

War Emergency Power Full power with water injection, producing the maximum amount of horsepower possible from the engine

Water injection Sprays water directly into the cylinder to cool certain parts of the induction system where "hot points" could produce premature ignition of the fuel/air mixture

Zeke Japanese Navy A6M Type Zero fighter

ZOI Zone of the Interior (continental US)

Zoom climb Tactic of using a dive to increase speed that can then be translated into higher altitude using the dive's energy to facilitate a faster climb

Acknowledgments and Picture Credits

As with any project of this magnitude, no one "goes it alone." I owe a deep debt of gratitude to Air Force Historian Yvonne Kinkaid. Yvonne's amazing ability to locate the exact page out of hundreds of microfilm reels and thousands of pages of documentation rescued me on more than one occasion. The families of these amazing aviators have been extremely supportive as well. Doug Patteson, Robert Hollowell, Scott Dennison, and Anita DiStefano, thank you for sharing your loved ones—that connection makes writing about these remarkable men that much more real. To my fellow historians Roger Connor, Nigel Julian, Peter Randall, Syd Edwards, Gerald Asher, Norris Graser, James William Marshall, Stephen Fowler, Steve Donacik—our endless hours of discussion of one particular photo or another has made this volume far better. Zane Mohler, Dustin Roderigas, Brian Benedict, and Mark Jones for their generous assistance and use of memorabilia. And Roy and Irene Grinnell; Roy for his constantly spectacular artwork, and Irene for being a phenomenal sounding board for ideas. I look forward to working with you both again! And the Fort Sill Director of Museums, Mr. Frank Siltman, for always being supportive of his museum directors, whether they are working on museum projects or something extracurricular. That support has been a blessing.

I want to thank my wife and my boys, who put up with Daddy's crazy hours, messy workspace, and constant monopolization of the family computer. And lastly, I'd like to dedicate this book to my father-in-law and fellow airplane lover, Paul Dyson, who was so supportive as I started out on this project, but left us far too soon. We miss you Paul.

Picture Credits

Page number and position are indicated as follows: L = left; R = right; TL = top left; TR = top right; C = center; CL = center left; B = bottom; BL = bottom left, etc.

US Air Force collection: 12, 14, 16, 17R, 19, 20, 21B, 22, 30T, 37, 38B, 39T, 40, 41R, 42B, 43, 44, 46T, 46B, 47L, 48B, 49T, 49B, 50, 51T, 52B, 54T, 55, 56, 58L, 58R, 59T, 60T, 60B, 61B, 63T, 65B, 66B, 70BL, 70BR, 71C, 71B, 72T, 72B, 73L 74, 75B, 76, 77L, 77R, 78T, 78B, 80, 84B, 85T, 86B, 89, 91R, 92, 96, 97B, 98, 99T, 102, 103T, 103C, 104, 105L, 105R, 106T, 106C, 106B, 107B, 109R, 110L, 111T, 112, 113L, 113R, 114, 115L, 115R, 118B, 119C, 119B, 120, 121TR, 124B, 125L, 126B, 127L, 127R, 127C, 128, 130T, 130B, 131C, 131B, 133T, 134L, 134R, 135R, 137, 138L, 139R, 140, 142TL, 142TR, 142R, 143R, 144L, 146B, 147T, 147B, 147TL, 147BL, 150CL, 150CR, 151BR

Author's collection: 15L, 15C, 21T, 23T, 23C, 24T, 31b, 31L, 31R, 33TL, 33TR, 34L, 34R, 34B, 38TC, 41BC, 42TC, 47B, 48T, 53, 55, 59C, 61, 62, 64L, 64R, 65, 66, 67T, 67B, 67C, 71, 73R, 75TL, 75TR, 75C, 79R, 82T, 82B, 83T, 83B, 84C, 85B, 86T, 87T, 88B, 90B, 94L, 94R, 94B, 95L, 95C, 97L, 97R, 98C, 98B, 99C, 99B, 101T, 101L, 108, 110T, 110R, 111C, 119T, 121, 122, 123, 124T, 125R, 133B, 134T, 135L, 138R, 143T, 144, 146T, 148T, 148L, 148B, 149C, 149R, 149C, 149BR, 150T, 151T

Air Defense Artillery Museum: 24B, 39C, 103R, 106C, 126C, 131T, 139, 143B, 145

Bob Hanning via Mark O'Boyle: 70T

Doug Patteson: 132T, 132C

Jean Barbaud: 109T

Jeff Ethell Collection: 68

Mark Barry: 139L

Mark Jones: 115T

National Air & Space Museum: 32B

Nigel Julian and Peter Randall: 116, 118TC, 121CL, 121BR, 122R, 123L, 123R, 126T,

Pat Bunce: 26, 27, 28, 29T, 29B, 30B, 31T, 32T, 33B, 35

Rob Hollowell: 67BL, 90T, 91L

Roger Freeman Collection: 53, 87B, 148BR

Steve Donacik: 95R, 103B,

Tyler Emery: 25, 79, 88T

Jacket and front cover illustration:
Roy Grinnell, Artist of the Aces
Website: *www.roygrinnell.com*